DECORATING CAKES AND PARTY FOODS
Baking Too!

Decorating Cakes and Party Foods
Baking Too!

by Louise Spencer

photography by Bob Dickstein

HEARTHSIDE PRESS, INCORPORATED

PUBLISHERS   •   NEW YORK

Dedicated to my students, whose enthusiasm for learning

has been my greatest reward for teaching

CONTENTS

Foreword

This book was written with the homemaker in mind. Throughout my years of teaching I have seen how much love was behind the desire to learn to do things that would bring pleasure to family and friends. I have remembered the smiles at the first successful attempt at making a perfect flower and the stories about the delight of some child or elderly person at receiving a decorated birthday cake. These are some of the things that have prompted me to write this book.

In addition to the decorating instructions, I have attempted to answer the questions most frequently asked of me and to eliminate certain difficulties you may encounter, by calling them to your attention, and telling you how to anticipate and correct them. All through the book I've tried to bring you the best possible methods, and, where advisable, easier alternates to use until you master the more advanced ones. This is done so that even your first attempts, though simple, will be successful. These alternatives, however, are not meant to be used on a continuing basis. I hope you will use them only in the beginning. They are not a substitute for practice, because only through practice will you attain any degree of proficiency in this fascinating art.

All of the cakes and foods pictured in this volume were prepared in my own kitchen, using standard decorating tools and utensils found in the average home. The only unusual piece of equipment I have used which may not be found in all homes is a heavy-duty mixer, which enables me to handle unusually large quantities of batter.

With a little patience and practice, you will be able to duplicate any cake or food design in this book, while gradually incorporating ideas of your own. In the beginning you may work slowly; this is natural. Strive for neatness first; speed will come in time, and the good habit of working neatly will remain.

It is my sincere wish that this book and the knowledge you gain from it will bring as much pleasure to you and your loved ones as my decorating has brought to my family, friends and to me over the years.

Louise Spencer

Acknowledgments

My sincere thanks to everyone who helped by word or deed to make this book a reality.

Special thanks are in order to Bob Dickstein for the lovely color transparencies, Wolly's, Incorporated and Birkentall Florists, for their many kindnesses, and to Colonial Studios of White Plains, New York for their permission to use the poodle picture duplicated on one of the cakes.

Last, but certainly not least, my thanks to Nedda Anders and her staff at Hearthside Press, and my devoted husband and daughters; without their help and encouragement I could never have been equal to the task.

Chapter 1

AN INTRODUCTION TO BAKING

Most cake decorators prefer to bake their own cakes from fresh ingredients or sometimes from prepared mixes, but a few decorators do buy their cakes. The important thing is to be realistic about your ability to make a good one. If you don't enjoy home baking, use a fine bought product, keeping in mind that frosting won't conceal poor flavor or texture. Although well-decorated cakes are expensive, the difference in price between first- and second-rate cakes is negligible. A good cake begins with fresh ingredients.

About Ingredients and Substitutions

BAKING POWDER: Double-acting baking powder is used in all our recipes. To substitute a tartrate or phosphate type, use 1½ teaspoons for every teaspoon of double-acting baking powder used in the recipe. Sprinkle tartrate or phosphate baking powder over the batter during the last minute of mixing time; bake immediately. Note: To test any baking powder for freshness stir a teaspoonful into half a glass of hot water. If it does not bubble actively discard it and buy another can.

BUTTER OR MARGARINE: Where butter is specified in the frostings or cakes, I prefer sweet butter, but salt butter may be substituted. Margarine will give a texture similar to that of butter, but not its flavor. Do *not* use the whipped butter or margarines; they would introduce too much air into the frostings.

1 stick = ½ cup butter (¼ pound)
2 sticks = 1 cup butter (½ pound)

CHOCOLATE: 3 tablespoons of cocoa and 1 tablespoon of shortening may be used in place of 1 square (1 ounce) of unsweetened chocolate.

15

CONFECTIONERS' SUGAR: Cornstarch is the ingredient in confectioners' sugar which prevents caking. A variation in cornstarch content may affect the consistency of the frosting. For this reason, you may find it necessary to add a bit of extra sugar or liquid to produce the ideal consistency for spreading or piping the frosting on to the cake.

CORN SYRUP: Light or dark corn syrup can be used interchangeably except where color may be a factor.

EGGS: Unless otherwise specified, medium eggs are used in all the recipes in this book.

EGG WHITES: 1½ teaspoons of meringue powder and 1¾ tablespoons of water may be used for each egg white called for in the frosting and icing recipes in this book. (See Sources of Supply)

FLOUR: All-purpose and cake flours are more or less interchangeable, but cake flour produces a more delicate texture (not necessarily an asset in decorated cakes, where firmness is desirable). Substitute as follows:

For one cup cake flour use ⅞ cup all-purpose flour

For 1 cup all-purpose flour use 1⅛ cups cake flour

MILK: May be fresh, or evaporated mixed with equal parts of water. To substitute sweet milk for sour milk add 1 teaspoon vinegar or lemon juice to each cup. To use sour milk in place of sweet milk add 1 teaspoon baking soda to each cup.

PIPING GEL: A clear gel with a faint citrus flavor made from agar is used in cake decorating in many ways. Its softness makes it ideal for inscriptions as it flows smoothly from the parchment cone or decorating tube. Leaves and flowers made from gel are pretty but quite flat since the consistency is not stiff enough to make them stand. Its glass-like transparency makes possible realistic stained glass windows, vases, etc. on cakes.

Small tubes of colored gel are available in food markets. It also comes in 2½- and 5-pound cans, colored or uncolored. I prefer to color it myself using paste colors. I keep small covered containers (about 1 cupful) colored and ready for use when needed. Piping gel requires no refrigeration; store in a cool dry place. (See Sources of Supply.)

SHORTENING: The hydrogenated type (packed in 1-pound and 3-pound cans) is used in the recipes in this book. *Do not* substitute the whipped or fluffed types.

SUGAR: Granulated sugar is used in all the recipes unless confectioners' sugar is specified. (See note under Confectioners' sugar.)

VANILLA: Pure vanilla extract is used in all recipes except when the slight color it imparts is undesirable, as in wedding cake frosting. To keep frostings white, use colorless vanilla. (See Sources of Supply.)

About Pans

Cakes baked in layers and sheets are the most popular of all. Layer cakes are usually the choice for family parties and small gatherings, and they are a *must* if a filling is desired. Sheet cakes are used chiefly when a large group is to be served, because they are easier to cut. Also because they are only one layer deep, they can be cut into small pieces.

Basic cake shapes—round, square or rectangle—can be decorated for any occasion with appropriate designs; if you are just starting out, I would suggest that you buy pans in simple geometric shapes.

Which pans to buy?

Before buying any pan larger than 12″, measure your oven. It should be at least 1½″ longer and wider than the pan.

My own collection consists mostly of tier pans which can be used for layer cakes, but are also deep enough to use for the higher layers necessary in making tier cakes. Layer cake pans are generally 1″ to 1½″ deep, while tier pans range from 2½″ deep to 4″ deep. They are available in sizes from 6″ to 16″ increasing in increments of 1″ so any size or combination of sizes is possible. I have had good results baking as little as 1″ of batter in these deeper pans. In some instances, as with the 10″ round pan, I use extra batter and bake a thicker cake which I then split and fill for a two-layer cake.

To help you decide which pans to purchase, I have listed all sizes and shapes used in this book; those I use most are marked with an asterisk. Some of these pans are shown in figure 1.

ROUND PANS

6″, 7″, 8″—Used primarily as top tiers on wedding cakes; the 8″ one is good for a small layer cake.

9″ and *10″—Perfect for family-size layer cakes. Also used in tier cakes. I use the 10″ size most.

11″ to 16″—Used individually for layer cakes; also in tier cakes.

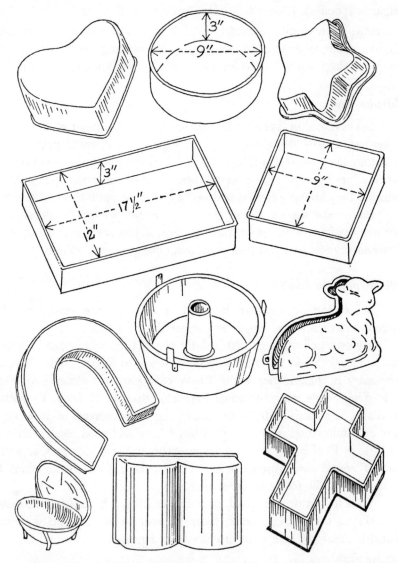

Fig. 1. Standard baking pans include the round (first row center), rectangle or square (second row), and tube (third row center); most are available in 8″, 9″ or 10″ sizes. The loaf pan (not shown) is basic too. Some special-occasion cakes can be cut from standard pans (see fig. 2).

SQUARE PANS

6", 7", 8"—Same as round pans.

*9" to 16"—May be used as sheet cakes, layer cakes, or tier cakes.

RECTANGULAR PANS

*12" x 17½" x 3"—I bake sheet cakes 1½" high so I prefer this pan to one with less depth. I have found also that the shallow pans (1" deep) tend to warp slightly from oven heat causing the batter to flow to the opposite corner, resulting in an uneven cake.

8" x 14" x 3" for smaller sheet cakes. Interchangeable with 9" x 13" pan but preferable to it because it has straight sides.

9" x 13"—Same as above.

10" x 15" x 1"—Jelly roll pan.

TUBE PANS are best used for angel food, pound and chiffon cakes. The hole in the center can be covered with a small piece of cardboard before the cake is frosted if you want an unbroken top surface (of course, you'll have to remove the cardboard or slice around it to serve), but for some designs the hole in the center is an asset. It could hold a nosegay of fresh or frosting flowers, or a tiny glass for warmed brandy, to be flamed at the table.

SPECIAL OCCASION PANS

If you have money and storage space aplenty, or want them for professional reasons, you may add some of the following:

Book pans: 10" x 14" x 3"—The most versatile of the special pans. For religious occasions, birthdays, anniversaries, children's cakes, etc. Also available in 8" x 12" x 3" size. (A book can be cut from a rectangular cake; see fig. 2.)

Heart pans: Various sizes, for bridal showers, engagement parties, Valentine's Day cakes, etc. A heart may also be cut from a square and a round cake.

Cross or Star-of-David pan: To use for religious occasions; can also be cut from a square or round cake.

Lamb, rabbit, clown, horseshoe, chicken, egg, etc.: 1- and 2-piece molds for children's parties, holidays, etc. These need a heavy pound-cake type batter.

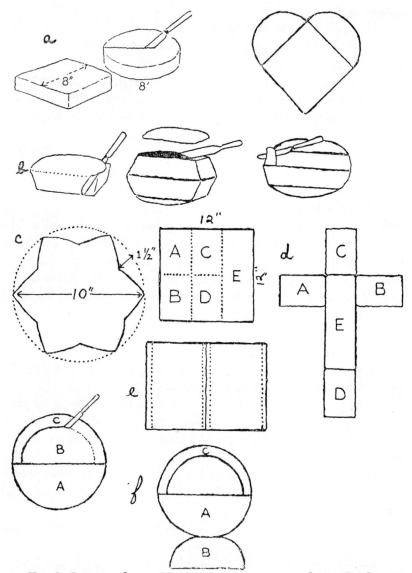

Fig. 2. Cutout cakes. a *Heart cut from square and round cakes. 30 slices.* b *Rounded tops cut from two 9" x 5" x 3" loaf cakes. Frost 4 sections together, trim to egg shape; frost completely. 12 slices.* c *For Star-of-David, mark round cake with toothpicks, cut away 6 points. 16 pieces.* d *Cross, cut from 12" square sheet, makes 40 slices.* e *Book from 9" x 13" cake. Slit at solid center line about ⅓ through. Slant cuts at dotted lines for "page" effect. 30 pieces.* f *Basket cut from 10" round cake. 12-16 pieces.*

Cut-out Cakes

Cake pans are available in a great many shapes and the proper pan makes the job a great deal easier, but here are some ideas you might like to use until you acquire all those special pans. To obtain best results with the picture cakes, follow the simple steps below.

1. Bake the cake at least one day before cutting, or freeze cake and cut while still frozen.

2. Use a very sharp knife, preferably one with a serrated edge.

3. Leave the crust on as much of the cake as possible. The crust should, however, be trimmed from pieces of cake to be joined together. Spread frosting on both edges to be joined and press firmly together.

4. Give entire assembled cake a thin coat of frosting to set the crumbs.

5. Allow to stand at least 4 hours before applying the finish coat of frosting.

When baking in glass pans

Glass conducts heat very quickly so if you are baking in glass pans set the temperature 25° lower than the setting specified in the recipe.

Adapting recipes to pans of varied sizes

Most of our cake recipes can be adapted to pans of different sizes and shapes, since we give batter yield. The amount listed below will fill pans from ½ to ⅔ of capacity, which is about right.

ROUND PANS

     6″ pan—1¼ cups batter
     7″ pan—1¾ cups batter
     8″ pan—2¼ cups batter
     9″ pan—2½ cups batter
     10″ pan—3½ cups batter
     11″ pan—4¼ cups batter
     12″ pan—5¾ cups batter
     13″ pan—7 cups batter
     14″ pan—8 cups batter
     15″ pan—9½ cups batter
     16″ pan—11 cups batter

SQUARE PANS

     6″ pan—2½ cups batter

8" pan—3½ cups batter
10" pan—6 cups batter
12" pan—9 cups batter
14" pan—14 cups batter
16" pan—17 cups batter

TUBE PANS

9" pan—5 cups batter
10" pan—10 cups batter (for chiffon cake)

OTHER

8" x 13" x 2"—5 cups batter
8" x 14" x 3"—5 or 6 cups batter
9" x 13" x 2"—5 cups batter
8" x 12" book cake pan—7 to 8 cups batter
10" x 10" x 3"—6 cups batter
10" x 14" book cake pan—14 to 15 cups batter
15" x 4" x 4" pan—10 to 11 cups batter
12" x 17½" x 3"—11 to 12 cups batter for sheet or single layer cake

TO MEASURE THE CAPACITY OF ODD-SHAPED PANS

Follow manufacturer's suggestion as to amount of batter to use, or measure the capacity of the mold as follows: If mold is baked uncovered, fill with water, measuring each cup. Use only ⅔ the amount of batter as water capacity. To measure the capacity of two-piece molds, which are baked covered, fill the bottom half with water. *Use as much batter as water*, filling the mold to the very top, because the batter can expand to fill the upper part of the mold.

Preparing pans

HOW TO GREASE PANS

Spread a coating of fat (oil, shortening, butter, etc.) to cover the inside of the pan using the fingertips, a pastry brush or a piece of crumpled paper.

HOW TO FLOUR PANS

Sprinkle about 2 tablespoons flour into the greased pan, shake to spread, tap the pan sharply on a solid surface, and pour off any loose flour. If the entire surface is not coated, you'll know that some parts were not greased. Dab a bit of shortening on these spots and sprinkle with flour. Remove excess.

HOW TO LINE THE BOTTOM OF PANS

In my experience, any 10" pan or larger should be lined on the bottom to eliminate the possibility that the cake will break when it is removed. Wax paper or release paper (see Sources of Supply) may be used as a liner. Grease the pan as directed in the recipe, then line it as follows: Trace the outline of the bottom of the pan on the paper as close to the edge as possible. (A pencil may be used as the marks will be cut away.) Cut out the paper slightly inside the marks to compensate for the difference between the outside and inside measurement of the pan. Press the liner into the pan and smooth with the fingers.

If the pan is very large it may be necessary to piece the liner. Overlap the edges of the paper about ½ inch. Spread a bit of shortening between the overlapped edges and press smooth with hands to prevent batter from seeping between them. Do not line springform pans unless specified in the recipe.

About Baking and Cooling Cake

How to space the pans

When using more than one oven rack stagger the pans, (not one above the other) so that air circulates all around. Never allow the pans to touch each other or the side of the oven.

How to adjust temperature and baking time

Baking times are approximate because ovens vary. No one knows your oven the way you do. Check the cake after the shortest baking time given, especially if your oven overheats. If you doubt the accuracy of the oven thermostat, have it checked or use an oven thermometer to control oven heat. Always check cake with a cake tester to be sure it is done before removing it from the oven. (Some cakes do not spring back when touched lightly with the finger even if ready.)

How to retard browning in large cakes

To keep large or very thick cakes from browning too soon place a shallow pan of water on a rack below it while the cake is baking. Remove the water when the cake is nearly baked to allow browning.

How to cool cakes

Allow cakes to cool in the pan on a rack for the specified time before removing from the pan. If after the cake has been loosened around the edges it is still stuck to the pan, turn it over on a rack. Wet a small towel in very hot water, wring out some of the excess water, and place over the bottom and sides of the pan. Allow to stand for a few minutes to create steam between the cake and the bottom of the pan.

If you do not have a rack large enough for a cake, use an oven rack. Be sure the rack is cool before putting the cake on it. Prop the corners of the rack with saucers to keep it above the work surface so that air will circulate under the cake.

If the bottom of the pan was lined with paper, remove it as soon as the cake is turned out of the pan. Gently lift the paper away from the outside edges first, then pull it straight across to remove it without breaking the cake. *Do not* allow the cake to become cold before attempting to remove the paper.

Always cool cakes top side up on the racks.

About Freezing Cake

All types of cakes may be frozen successfully if a few simple rules are observed. Unfrosted cakes will keep up to 5 months if stored at zero degrees. Frosted cakes should be used within 3 months. Buttercreams or confectioners' sugar frostings freeze well on cakes, but do not attempt to freeze cakes iced with boiled or seven-minute type icings.

TO PREPARE CAKES FOR FREEZING, bake as usual and cool thoroughly. Place on a commercial cake board or a piece of heavy cardboard covered with aluminum foil or plastic wrap. Follow directions below.

Freezing plain cakes

Prepare as described above and wrap in freezer wrap. Seal airtight with freezer tape. To thaw let stand at room temperature without unwrapping for about 3 hours.

TO FROST AND DECORATE cakes after they have thawed, unwrap and let stand uncovered until all condensation on the surface evaporates completely, as frosting will not adhere properly to a wet surface. Frost and decorate as desired.

Freezing frosted cakes

Place on cake board and freeze unwrapped until frosting is firm. Remove from freezer, wrap in freezer wrap and seal with freezer tape. Return to freezer until needed. To thaw, unwrap immediately and place under cake cover or large bowl to retain moisture.

Freezing decorated cakes

I prefer to bake and decorate a cake one or two days before it is to be served rather than run the risk of having decorations damaged while the cake is in the freezer, but this is not always possible. Decorated cakes should be placed in cake boxes to protect them. Seal the box with freezer tape or wrap the entire box in freezer paper first, then seal. To thaw, allow the cake to remain in the box at room temperature for about 3 hours.

Cakes that have been frozen will dry out faster than freshly baked ones. For small families it may be best to cut cakes into halves or quarters and wrap each piece individually before freezing. In this way only as much cake as is wanted need be defrosted at one time.

As with all baking, only the finest ingredients should be used in cakes to be frozen. It is especially important to use only pure extracts for flavoring. Imitation flavorings, though stronger at the time they are used, lose fragrance and flavor in freezing.

Freezing unbaked batter is not recommended.

Cake Failures: Problems and Solutions

A. Sponge or angel food cakes:

For leavening, cakes of this type depend on the air beaten into the eggs or egg whites; they contain no fat. The causes of failure and methods of prevention (note, I did not promise "cures"; except that you can slice off sections of a cake to make it level, or add slices where needed), are:

1. CAKE IS TIGHT-GRAINED AND UNDERSIZED
    a. Egg whites not at room temperature when beaten
    b. Ingredients not folded together gently enough; air allowed to escape from batter
    c. Oven too hot; thermostat could be at fault here
    d. Pan too large for recipe

  e. Cake not allowed to hang until completely cold before removal from pan, causing the tiny air cells to collapse and become compact

2. TEXTURE OF CAKE IS COARSE, UNEVEN, OR RUBBERY
  a. Egg whites not beaten long enough
  b. Ingredients not folded together thoroughly
  c. Oven too hot or too cold

3. CRUST TOO HARD OR STICKY
  a. Oven too hot
  b. Baking time inaccurate
  c. Too much sugar used

Angel food cakes are baked in a tube pan because the core assures better penetration of heat through the batter. Sponge cakes are baked in tube pans, but may be baked in layers or sheets as well.

B. Butter cakes:

Cakes in this category do contain fat (butter, margarine or shortening) and depend upon baking powder or baking soda for leavening. Possible type of failure, together with their usual causes, are as follows:

1. CAKE SINKS IN THE MIDDLE
  a. Too much sugar, shortening or leavening
  b. Moving cake before batter has set
  c. Slamming oven door while batter is still in soft state
  d. Excessive amount of egg white used in recipe
  e. Oven not hot enough
  f. Cake not baked long enough

2. TEXTURE OF CAKE IS COARSE
  a. Shortening, shortening and sugar, or shortening, sugar and eggs not creamed to proper stage (light, fluffy etc.)
  b. Excessive amount of leavening used
  c. Insufficient amount of sugar used
  d. Egg whites not folded in thoroughly, which would only apply where they are added separately
  e. In cakes where baking soda is used a few larger holes in an otherwise even texture may be expected
  f. Not scraping bowl and beaters enough during mixing, which is especially true in cakes made from packaged mixes

g. Oven not preheated long enough to attain proper temperature before cake was put in to bake (Allow at least 10 min- for preheating.)

3. CAKE IS DRY
   a. Overbaking
   b. Temperature of oven too low
   c. Not enough shortening used
   d. Flour improperly measured resulting in too much being used
   e. Too much leavening

4. CAKE IS UNDERSIZED
   a. Too large a pan used
   b. Ingredients too cold
   c. Insufficient amount of leavening used
   d. Oven too hot
   e. Batter not mixed thoroughly

5. CRACKS IN TOP OF CAKE
   a. Too much flour
   b. Overmixing of batter
   c. Oven too hot

6. CAKE IS TOUGH
   a. Too little sugar or shortening
   b. Too much flour
   c. Oven not preheated long enough before cake was put in to bake

7. CAKE STICKS TO BOTTOM OF PAN
   a. Allowed to stand too long in pan before removing
   b. Pan not greased enough
   c. Too much liquid
   d. Batter underbeaten
   e. Oven temperature too low

8. CRUST ON CAKE VERY DARK
   a. Baked in metal pan which has become dark from long use or improper cleaning
   b. Glass pan used in place of metal pan and temperature not reduced 25° F.

9. CAKE NOT LEVEL
   a. Oven racks not level

  b. Uneven oven heat

  c. Pans touching each other or sides of the oven

10. EXCESSIVE SHRINKING OF CAKE

  a. Oven too hot

  b. Ingredients too warm; most likely to happen during summer or in warm climates. Use eggs and milk directly from the refrigerator

  c. Overbaked

11. TOP CRUST MOIST AND STICKY

  a. Too much sugar, too much liquid, or both

12. CAKE IS CRUMBLY

  a. Batter overbeaten or underbeaten

  b. Not enough egg used

  c. Excessive amount of shortening or leavening used

  d. Cake put into oven before it had preheated to proper temperature

Butter cakes may be baked in pans of many shapes. Pound cakes baked in very large pans to be used for wedding cake tiers benefit from having a removable core (see Sources of Supply) placed in the center of the pan before the batter is placed into it. This core helps heat to penetrate evenly throughout the batter.

C. Butter-sponge cakes:

These, being a combination of sponge and butter cake, rely for leavening on the air beaten into the eggs or egg white—but they also contain fat. Genoise and Chiffon cakes fall into this category. These cakes are subject to the same kinds of failure as Angel Food and Sponge Cakes, but can also fail because of excess flour. The best warranty for success with butter sponge cakes is to thoroughly understand all possible causes of cake failure.

How to insure level cakes

To get cakes that don't hump in the middle, use the following method: Cut strips of terry cloth (old towels are fine) about three times as wide as the depth of the pan. For example, if the pan is 3″ deep you would cut the strips 9″ wide. The strip should be long enough to go all around the outside of the pan, so seam pieces together if necessary. Wet the strip and wring out the excess water; it should be wet but not dripping. Fold in three lengthwise and pin tightly around the outside of the pan. Grease the pan or prepare as you normally would and bake as usual. I do not recommend this method for angel food cakes but it works like a charm on cakes made from packaged mixes, and on pound and butter cakes. It is especially helpful on square and rectangular cakes, which tend to bake too fast in the corners and become very dark and brittle, while the centers rise so high it is necessary to cut the cakes to level them.

Adjusting recipes for high altitude baking

OVEN TEMPERATURE: At all altitudes over 3,500 feet, increase oven temperature 25 degrees.

FLOUR: At 3,500 feet add 1 tablespoon more flour and then add one tablespoon more for each 1,500 foot increase in elevation above 3,500 feet.

EGGS: Use maximum number of eggs called for in the recipes. If part of egg is needed to make full measure, add egg whites—not yolk.

SUGAR: Do not reduce at any altitude.

LEAVENING: Larger amounts of leavening are required at lower altitudes, less at higher altitudes. If recipe calls for baking powder, soda or both adjust as follows per teaspoonful required in the recipe:

> 2,000 to 3,000 ft., use only ¾–⅔ teaspoon
> 3,500 to 5,000 ft., use only ⅔–½ teaspoon
> 5,000 to 6,500 ft., use only ½–⅓ teaspoon
> 6,500 to 8,000 ft., use only ⅓–¼ teaspoon

GREASE AND FLOUR CAKE PANS THOROUGHLY. (Cakes have a tendency to stick to the pan at high altitudes.) Use a high grade vegetable shortening. Measure accurately and bake exactly as directed.

ANGEL FOOD AND SPONGE CAKES: Beat egg whites only to a soft peak. Fold in dry ingredients lightly and quickly using as few strokes as possible.

About Mixing

Before starting to mix

1. Assemble all ingredients. Allow time for ingredients to come to room temperature (about 1 hour).
2. Preheat oven about 10 to 15 minutes.

3. Measure ingredients accurately using standard measuring cups and spoons. Flour should be spooned lightly into the measuring cup. Brown sugar should be packed tightly. Use the straight edge of a knife to level tops of cupfuls and spoonfuls.
4. Prepare pans according to instructions in the recipe (grease or grease and flour, line with paper, etc.). Cakes baked in pans greased with butter will have a somewhat tastier crust than with shortening but will be more difficult to remove from pans. For this reason, I prefer to grease pans with shortening.

How to cream ingredients

Work ingredients with a wooden paddle, rotary beater or an electric mixer until they are soft, creamy and well blended. The stage to which ingredients are to be creamed (light, fluffy, like whipped cream, etc.) is specified in each recipe. Always follow these instructions exactly, as the texture of the cake is greatly influenced by this step in the mixing.

How to fold ingredients

The term *folding* refers to the process of adding egg whites, whipped cream, melted chocolate, etc. to a batter in such a way as to incorporate air. Use a rubber spatula or a wooden paddle. Move the spatula down vertically to the bottom of the bowl. Continue across the bottom, then return to the surface and across the top, bringing some of the batter up from the bottom and folding it under at the top. Folding should be done thoroughly to combine ingredients properly but it should also be done gently so as not to remove any air from the mixture.

When the recipe calls for liquid and dry ingredients to be added alternately, always start and end with dry ingredients.

How to mix large amounts of batter

Most electric cake mixers can handle no more than 12 cups of batter at one time. If you need a larger quantity, prepare two batches of batter. Pour the first batch into the prepared pan and refrigerate it. Mix the second batch, pour it over the first one, and bake as directed. However, if cake is more than 12″ reduce the oven temperature by 25°.

Chapter 2

CAKE AND COOKIE RECIPES

Basically, there are three kinds of cakes that lend themselves to decoration—butter (shortening); sponge and angel; and butter-sponge cakes which include genoise and chiffon cakes. There are several different methods of blending ingredients; many choices of flavorings, frostings and fillings, and countless shapes into which cakes can be baked or cut. In short the variations are endless.

The recipes which follow are the ones most often used by my students; they are practically failure-proof, even for beginners.

Basic Sponge Cake

Preheat oven to 325° F.
One 8″ x 14″ x 3″ sheet pan,
   or one 9″ tube pan,
   or two 9″ round cake pans;
   do not grease.

5 eggs, separated	1 cup sifted cake flour
1 cup granulated sugar	¼ teaspoon salt
1 tablespoon lemon juice	

Beat eggs whites until they stand up in soft peaks (you'll get greater volume if the eggs are at room temperature). Beat in, a tablespoonful at a time, about ¼ cup of the granulated sugar. Continue beating until the mixture is stiff—about 5 minutes with an electric beater on medium. In another bowl, beat the yolks with 1 tablespoon lemon juice until thick and lemon-colored. Gradually beat in the remaining ¾ cup sugar. Pour this mixture over the whites and fold them gently together with a wooden spoon. Sprinkle flour and salt over the egg mixture and fold gently together until no peaks of beaten egg white can be seen. Spoon into the ungreased tube pan or layer cake pans and bake immediately for 15 to 20 minutes for the layers or up to 40 minutes for the sheet and tube. When the cake is golden brown and tests done (it should spring back if pressed lightly with the finger) remove from oven and let cool on rack, about an hour. Loosen cake with a spatula and ease out of pan. The cake may be decorated when completely cool, or held overnight and decorated the next day. Yield: 5 cups batter; 12-16 servings when decorated; 10-12 servings plain cake.

DECORATING NOTES: For a fluffier sponge cake, you may use an extra egg white or add from ½ up to 1½ teaspoons baking powder to the flour and salt. However, for decorating I prefer the firmer texture produced by the basic recipe.

Flavors may be varied almost without limit. You may add (or substitute for the lemon juice) 1 teaspoon grated orange rind or vanilla extract; or ½ teaspoon lemon, almond or anise extract. However, the frosting brings its own flavor so be sure the sponge cake does not overpower it.

This cake can be decorated several days after it is baked. It should stay moist and fresh if refrigerated or stored in a closed container for at least a week. It can be refrigerated after it is decorated without loss of texture.

Pound Cake

Do *not* preheat oven, bake at 350° F.
Grease and flour one 10″ tube pan.

2 cups sifted, self-rising cake flour	1 cup butter
1½ cups sugar	¾ cup milk
4 eggs	1 teaspoon vanilla extract

Combine all ingredients in mixing bowl and beat at medium speed 20 minutes, or until completely blended. Scrape bowl and beaters often. Pour into prepared pan and bake immediately for about 1 hour. *Start in a cold oven.* Cool on cake rack in pan for 10 minutes. Turn out of pan and place top side up on a rack until completely cool (about 1 hour). Sprinkle with sifted confectioners' sugar if desired. Yield: 5 cups batter; 16-20 servings.

DECORATING NOTE: The surprise here is a moistness not usually associated with pound cake. Couple this with a rich buttery flavor and you have a cake delectable enough to serve with only a sprinkling of confectioners' sugar, or a simple top frosting of Orange or Lemon Icing (see Index).

Marble Pound Cake

Divide Pound Cake batter into two parts. Melt 1½ squares chocolate and add to one part. With a tablespoon, alternately spoon light and dark batters into prepared pan. Follow baking directions for Pound Cake.

FOR MARBLE NUT POUND CAKE replace chocolate with ¼ cup chopped nuts and 1 tablespoon dark molasses.

Old-Fashioned Pound Cake

Preheat oven to 300° F.
Grease and flour one 9″ tube pan
    or one 10″ tube pan.

1 cup butter	2 teaspoons vanilla extract
1⅔ cups sugar	¼ teaspoon mace (optional)
5 eggs	2 cups sifted, all-purpose flour

Cream butter and sugar. Beat the eggs in one at a time. Add vanilla and mace, beating at medium speed until blended. Reduce mixer speed to low and fold in flour a tablespoon at a time. Pour into prepared pan. Bake immediately about 1½ hours. Cool on cake rack 10 minutes before removing from pan. Cool about 1 hour before frosting or dusting with confectioner's sugar. Yield: 5 cups batter; 15-20 slices.

NOTE: This traditional pound cake is perfect for two-piece molds (lamb, bunny, etc.) because of its firm texture.

Variations

COCONUT CAKE

Add ¾ cup freshly grated coconut to batter. Frost with 1 recipe Boiled Icing (see Index) to which add 1 cup freshly grated coconut.

Use as filling and icing. Sprinkle ½ cup moist grated coconut over top while icing is still soft.

DUNDEE CAKE

Sprinkle on top before baking: 3 tablespoons mixed candied citron, and orange peel (or grated orange rind), and 1 cup mixed currants and sultana raisins.

SPICED POUND CAKE

Add ½ teaspoon nutmeg and ½ teaspoon mace to batter.

Genoise

Preheat oven to 350° F.
Grease and flour two 9″ round pans
  or one 8″ x 14″ x 3″ sheet pan.

½ cup butter	1 teaspoon vanilla extract
6 large eggs, separated	1 cup sugar
1 teaspoon grated lemon rind	1 cup sifted, all-purpose flour

Melt butter over low heat and set aside to cool. Combine egg yolks, lemon rind, and vanilla in bowl, beat at medium speed until blended. Place egg whites in large bowl and beat until they hold a soft peak. Add sugar gradually, beating thoroughly after each addition. Continue beating until a very stiff meringue is formed. Mix about ¼ of the meringue with the egg yolk mixture. Pour egg yolk and meringue mixture into the remaining meringue. Sift flour lightly over top and fold flour and egg mixture lightly together. Then add melted butter. Fold together gently only enough for flour and butter to disappear into the batter. Pour into prepared pans and bake immediately for 20 to 25 minutes. Allow cakes to stand in pans 4 minutes, then turn out onto racks to cool. Cool cakes right side up for about one hour. Yield: 5 cups batter; 12-16 servings decorated; 10-12 servings plain.

DECORATING NOTE: This most famous of all European butter-sponge cakes can be baked in loaf, round, square or sheet cake pans. After it has cooled it can be filled with fruit purée, jam or cream fillings or decorated with any favorite frostings. Like sponge cake, it is versatile and of almost perfect flavor and texture to harmonize with fillings and toppings.

Decorated Genoise with Mocha Filling

Split layers crosswise and sprinkle cut surfaces with Creme de Caçao liqueur. Put layers together with Mocha Filling (see Index) using bottom part of one layer, crust side up, at the top. Frost and border with Buttercream Frosting No. 1 or Chocolate Buttercream (see Index for recipes).

White Cake

Preheat oven to 350° F.
Grease and flour two 8″ round pans
  or one 10″ round pan 2½″ deep.

2 cups plus 2 tablespoons sifted,
  all-purpose flour
4 teaspoons baking powder
1 teaspoon salt
1½ cups sugar

½ cup shortening
1 cup milk
1 teaspoon vanilla extract
4 egg whites, unbeaten

Sift flour, baking powder, salt and sugar together into large bowl. Add shortening, milk and vanilla; beat at medium speed 2 minutes or until blended. Scrape bowl and beaters. Add egg whites and beat 1 minute. Scrape bowl and beaters. Beat for 1 minute longer. Bake for 30 to 35 minutes. Cool in pan(s) on cake rack 10 minutes. Turn out of pan(s), cool top side up about 1 hour before frosting. Batter may be kept in pans in refrigerator up to 3 hours before baking. Yield: about 5 cups batter; 12 generous servings or 16 smaller ones.

DECORATING NOTE: A versatile cake for almost any kind of filling or frosting. For a Strawberry Ice Cream Cake, fill layers (or cut loaf in half horizontally to make layers) with one-half gallon vanilla and strawberry ice cream. Purée 10 ounces frozen strawberries in blender; bring to boil. Dilute 1 tablespoon cornstarch in 3 tablespoons Kirsch liqueur; add to berries. Cook for a few minutes. Cool in refrigerator then spread on top and sides of cake. Serve with whipped cream and fresh berries or slightly thawed frozen berries.

Lady Baltimore Cake

Two 8″ layers White Cake
1 recipe Lady Baltimore Filling
  (see Index)

1 recipe Boiled Icing (see Index)

Fill cooled baked layers with Lady Baltimore Filling, and ice with Boiled Icing.

Sour Milk Chocolate Cake

Preheat oven to 350° F.
Grease bottoms and line with paper:
Two 9" round cake pans
    or one deep 10" round cake pan.

4 squares unsweetened chocolate, grated	2 cups sifted, all-purpose flour
½ cup shortening	1½ teaspoons baking soda
1 cup boiling water	mixed into ½ cup sour milk
2 cups sugar	2 eggs
	1½ teaspoons vanilla extract

Combine unsweetened chocolate, shortening and boiling water in mixing bowl; stir. Add sugar, flour, soda and sour milk, eggs and vanilla. Beat at medium speed for 2 minutes or until mixture is blended. Scrape bowl and beaters and beat 1 minute longer. Pour into prepared pans or pan and bake immediately for about 30 minutes in 9" pans or 45 minutes in deep 10" pan. Test with cake tester before removing from oven. Cool in pan(s) on racks 10 minutes, then turn out and remove paper from bottom(s). Turn cake(s) top side up on racks to cool (45 minutes to 1 hour). Yield: 4 cups batter; 12-16 servings.

DECORATING NOTE: This very dark Chocolate Cake is delicious frosted with Buttercream No. 1 or Chocolate Frosting (see Index). Or use Chocolate Buttercream as filling between layers, top with Chocolate Whipped Cream and decorate with curls of chocolate or chocolate chips. To make Chocolate Whipped Cream: whip together until stiff 1 cup heavy cream, ⅓ cup sifted confectioners' sugar, 2 tablespoons cocoa and 1 teaspoon vanilla extract.

Yellow Cake

Preheat oven to 350° F.
Grease bottom and line with wax paper:
One 12" x 12" x 3" pan.

3½ cups sifted all-purpose flour	2¼ cups sugar
1 teaspoon salt	4 eggs, unbeaten
4 teaspoons baking powder	2 teaspoons vanilla extract
1 cup shortening	1½ cups milk

Sift flour, salt and baking powder together and set aside. Combine shortening and sugar in large bowl and cream at medium speed until light and fluffy. Add eggs and vanilla and beat for 2 minutes or until thoroughly blended. Add dry ingredients alternately with milk, beating at low speed only long enough to blend after each addition. Pour batter into prepared pan and bake for about 50 minutes or until cake tester inserted in center comes out clean. Batter may be kept in pan in refrigerator up to 3 hours before baking.

Cool cake in pan on rack for 10 minutes, then loosen around the edges and turn out on rack. Remove paper from bottom; turn top side up on rack to cool completely before frosting. Yield: 8 cups of batter; about 30 servings.

Enriched Yellow Cake from a Mix

Preheat oven to 350° F.
Grease and line with paper:
One 11½" x 17" pan
 or muffin tins lined with fluted paper cups.

1 package (1 pound 2½ ounces) Yellow Cake Mix	2 egg whites, unbeaten
	Water
2 eggs	1 teaspoon vanilla

Pour cake mix into large bowl. Add eggs and vanilla. Place two egg whites in bottom of 1-cup measure. Add enough water to make 1 cup. Pour into bowl. If instructions on package list more liquid than one cup, add needed amount. Mix batter according to package directions, pour into prepared pan or pans, and bake as directed—usually about 15 to 20 minutes or until cake tester comes out clean. Cool cake in pan on rack for ten minutes, or as directed on package. Yield: 5½ cups batter; 10-12 servings.

DECORATING NOTE: This one-bowl cake may be cut into Petits Fours (see Index) or used as decorated cup cakes for a children's party. Or fill with Almond Cream Filling and frost with Creamy Frosting.

Butter Cake

Preheat oven to 350° F.
Grease bottom and line with paper:
Two 8″ round pans *and* two 10″ round pans
  or two 12″ round pans.

6 cups sifted cake flour	6 eggs
4 teaspoons baking powder	2 egg yolks
1½ teaspoons salt	1½ cups milk
2 cups butter	2 teaspoons orange extract
3½ cups sugar	2 teaspoons vanilla extract

Sift flour, baking powder and salt together and set aside. In large bowl of electric mixer, cream butter at medium speed until very light; add sugar gradually and beat well. Add eggs, egg yolks, orange and vanilla extracts. Continue to beat until very light and fluffy. Reduce mixer speed to low. Add dry ingredients in five portions, alternating with milk, beating only enough to blend after each addition. Fill prepared pans half full and bake, or store in refrigerator up to 3 hours before baking. Bake 12″ cakes about 45 minutes, 8″ or 10″ cakes 25 to 30 minutes or until a cake tester inserted in the center comes out clean. Cool cakes in pans on a rack for 10 minutes. Turn out of pans and remove paper from bottoms. Cool top side up on racks about 1 hour. Yield: 12 cups batter; 10 servings from two-layer 8″ cake; 12 from 10″ cake; 26 to 30 from 12″ cake.

DECORATING NOTE: I have baked this cake hundreds of times in the last 15 years. This is the recipe I choose for the wedding tier cake (unless, of course, the bride prefers another kind) and it always makes a happy marriage with whatever we use for filling, frosting, and decorating.

Ice Water Fudge Cake

Preheat oven to 350° F.
Grease bottoms and line with paper:
Three 8″ round layer cake pans
  or one 8″ x 14″ x 3″ pan.

¾ cup butter	1½ teaspoons vanilla extract
2¼ cups sugar	3 cups sifted cake flour
3 eggs	1½ teaspoons baking soda
3 1-ounce squares unsweetened	½ teaspoon salt
chocolate, melted	1¼ cups ice water

Stir butter to soften; gradually add sugar beating at medium speed 2 minutes or until light and fluffy. Add eggs one at a time, beating well after each. Blend in cooled chocolate and vanilla at low speed on mixer. Sift together flour, soda, and salt; add to creamed mixture alternately with ice water, beating at low speed about 30 seconds after each addition or until blended. Bake immediately for about 30 minutes for 8" cakes; about 45 minutes for 8"x14"x3" pan. Cool on rack in pan(s) 10 minutes. Turn out on racks, remove paper and cool top side up on racks about 45 minutes before filling and frosting. Yield: 6 cups batter; 12-16 servings of decorated cake.

DECORATING NOTE: For this feathery-textured cake use Marshmallow Frosting (see Index) between layers and as icing; or fill, frost and border with Chocolate Fudge Frosting (see Index); decorate as desired.

Devil's Food Cake

Preheat oven to 350° F.
Grease bottoms and line with paper:
Three 8" round pans
 or one 10" square pan.

1 cup butter	1½ teaspoons baking soda
1¾ cups brown sugar, packed	¼ teaspoon baking powder
3 eggs	¼ teaspoon salt
2 cups sifted, all-purpose flour	¾ cup sour milk
⅔ cup cocoa	1½ teaspoons vanilla extract

With electric mixer at medium speed cream butter until fluffy. Add brown sugar and beat until well blended. Beat eggs in one at a time. Sift flour, cocoa, baking soda, baking powder and salt together 3 times. Mix vanilla with sour milk and add alternately with dry ingredients, beating well after each addition. Pour into prepared pans or pan and bake immediately. Bake 8" layers 25 minutes and 10" cake 50 minutes or until cake tester inserted in the center comes out clean. Cool in pan on rack 10 minutes. Turn cake(s) out and remove paper from the bottom(s). Turn top side up on rack and cool completely. 10" cake may be split lengthwise into two layers. Yield: 7 cups of batter; 16 servings from 8" cakes, 24 from 10" cake.

DECORATING NOTE: Fill with Almond Cream Filling and frost with Chocolate Buttercream (see Index for recipes).

Basic Angel Food Cake

Preheat oven to 350° F.
One 10″ tube pan;
   do not grease.

1¼ cups sugar
1 cup sifted cake flour
1 cup egg whites (about 8 or 9)
¼ teaspoon salt

1¼ teaspoons cream of tartar
2 teaspoons vanilla extract
   or almond flavor

Sift sugar and flour together 4 times and set aside. Combine egg whites and salt in large mixing bowl, beat at medium speed until foamy. Add cream of tartar and continue to beat until egg whites stand in soft peaks. Stir in vanilla. Fold in flour-sugar mixture about 2 tablespoons at a time, blending gently but thoroughly. Carefully spoon batter into pan. Bake immediately for 50 minutes, then turn oven off but allow cake to remain in oven 10 minutes longer. Remove from oven and turn pan upside down until cake is cold, about 1 hour. If pan does not have legs, prop edges or insert tube into bottle or jar so cake will be suspended above table or work surface. When cold, loosen cake around edges and remove from pan. Yield: 4 cups batter; 12-16 servings. Use tined cake breaker or pull apart gently with two forks to serve.

DECORATING NOTE: To make a "You're an angel" cake—perhaps for a club function—increase the ingredients by one-quarter. Fill an ungreased 1-cup capacity ovenproof bowl or custard cup about ¾ full of batter. Bake remaining batter in 10″ tube pan as described previously. Bake small cake about 15 to 20 minutes. Cool both cakes.

Split large cake in half making two layers. Fill with Almond Cream Filling. Frost with Boiled Icing, reserving about 1 cup. (See Index for recipes.)

Follow instructions for Doll Cake (see Index) using the small cake, a 3″ or 4″ doll and the reserved cup of frosting. (Frosting may be left white or tinted if desired.) Press small wings cut from silver foil into the frosting at the back of the doll. Make a tiny halo from a piece of silver chenille stem and place on doll's head. Using a spatula or pancake turner, carefully set the angel doll cake on the center of the large cake covering the hole in the center. (The small doll, silver foil and chenille stem are available in stores where arts and crafts materials are sold.)

Basic Chiffon Cake

Preheat oven to 325° F.
One 10″ tube pan
   or two 9″ x 13″ x 2″ pans;
   do not grease.

2 cups sifted, all-purpose flour
1½ cups sugar
3 teaspoons baking powder
1 teaspoon salt
½ cup cooking or salad oil
  (not olive oil)

5 egg yolks, unbeaten
¾ cup water
2 teaspoons vanilla extract
1 cup (about 8) egg whites
½ teaspoon cream of tartar

Sift flour, sugar, baking powder and salt together 3 times. Make a well in center and add oil, egg yolks, water and vanilla. Beat at medium speed of electric mixer about 1 minute or until smooth.

In large mixing bowl, beat egg whites and cream of tartar together until very stiff. *Do not underbeat.* Pour egg yolk mixture gradually over stiffly beaten egg whites and fold together gently using a rubber spatula. Pour into pan and bake immediately, about 1 hour for the 10″ cake and 50 minutes for the 9″x13″x2″ cake. Test by pressing cake gently in the center with fingertip. It will spring back if cake is done.

Turn cake upside down and let it hang suspended above the work surface until cold. Loosen at edges and ease out of pan. (If pan does not have legs, prop edges with small saucers.) Yield: 10 cups batter; 16 servings from 10″ cake; 16-20 from 9″x13″x2″ cake.

DECORATING NOTE: Frost top or spread with Cookie Glaze (see Index).

Ice Cream Chiffon Cake

Cut a slice ¾″ thick from the top of Basic Chiffon Cake; set aside. Carefully hollow out remaining cake using a small sharp knife. Sprinkle inside of hollowed cake with 2 jiggers of rum, creme de cacao or chartreuse liqueur if desired. Fill cake with slightly softened ice cream, pressing gently into place with a spoon to pack tightly. Replace top slice of cake. If ice cream has softened considerably place cake in freezer for a short time before garnishing with whipped cream. Whip 1 cup heavy cream until stiff. Attach pastry tube No. 6 (star tube) to a bag or large paper cone. Fill with whipped cream and pipe rosettes or scrolls on top of cake. A shell border may be added if desired. Place cake in box or freezer wrap and seal. Store in freezer until serving time. One-half gallon of ice cream will fill the cake generously.

Fruit-Filled Chiffon Cake

Hollow Basic Chiffon Cake as described above. Gently shred the pieces of cake removed from the center. Measure 1 cup of cake pieces. Place in bowl and add 1 cup fresh or drained canned fruit, cut into pieces, (bananas or peaches are especially good). Whip and sweeten to taste 1 cup of heavy cream and fold into cake and fruit mixture. Use to fill cake, spreading evenly in hollowed shell. Replace top of cake; dust with confectioners' sugar or spread top with Chocolate Glaze. Refrigerate until serving time. Keep any leftover cake refrigerated.

Orange Chiffon Cake

Follow recipe for Basic Chiffon Cake but substitute 1 cup orange juice for water, and 1 tablespoon grated orange rind for vanilla extract.

NOTE: Chiffon cakes are light in texture, with less body than sponge cakes, although they belong to the same family. They are quite versatile and lend themselves to many different sauces, toppings and garnishes.

Cup Cakes

Preheat oven to 350° F.
Line muffin pans with fluted paper liners.

½ cup shortening	2 teaspoons baking powder
1 cup sugar	½ teaspoon salt
3 eggs	½ cup milk
1¾ cups sifted, all-purpose flour	1 teaspoon vanilla extract

Cream shortening, sugar and eggs together at medium speed. Mix and sift flour, baking powder and salt and add alternately with the milk to the first mixture. Add vanilla and beat 1 minute. Pour into muffin pans and bake 15 to 20 minutes. If desired, batter may be poured into muffin pan and refrigerated up to 3 hours before baking. Yield: About 5 cups batter; 20 cup cakes.

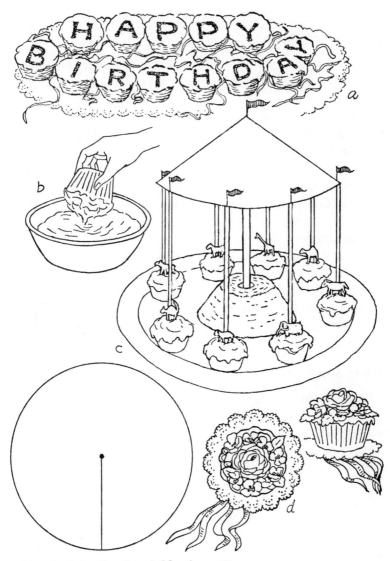

Fig. 3. Cupcakes for children's parties.

DECORATING NOTE: Frost with any favorite frosting. See figure 3 party decorations. For quick results, dip cup cakes into bowl of frosting. Turn wrist slightly.

Cupcake Carousel, fig. 3

1. Cut canopy from a circle of construction paper. Slash to center as shown. Overlap slashed edges, and staple together to form peak in center.

2. Bake center cake in bowl about 6″ in diameter. Bake 8 cupcakes in paper-lined muffin tins. When cool frost with Buttercream or Mock Marshmallow Frosting.

3. Cover 8 animal cookies with Cookie Glaze in appropriate colors.

4. Press large plastic drinking straw in center of bowl cake and in each cupcake. Trim a bit from top of cupcake straws (for different heights between the peak and side of canopy). Set canopy into place, resting on straws.

5. Cut 9 pennants from construction paper and fasten to toothpicks. Press ends of toothpicks through canopy and into straws below.

6. Put a dab of frosting at center back of each animal cookie. Press upright on cupcakes as shown, leaning them against the straws for support. The frosting at the back will help hold them against the straws. (See Fig 3c.)

Nosegay Cupcakes

Frost and decorate top of cupcake with piped flower (mum, daffodil, rose). Pipe drop flowers or No. 30 rosettes around center; add leaves with cut parchment cone (fig. 19). Serve on small paper doily to which ribbon streamers have been fastened with a dab of frosting, fig. 3d.

Cake For French Pastry

Preheat oven to 360° F.
Grease bottom and line with paper:
One 17" x 11½" x 1" pan.

1¼ cups sifted cake flour	¼ cup plus 2 tablespoons butter
¾ cup plus 2 tablespoons sugar	2 eggs
2¼ teaspoons baking powder	2 teaspoons vanilla
½ teaspoon salt	½ cup milk

Sift flour, sugar, baking powder and salt together into large bowl of electric mixer. Add the butter, eggs and vanilla extract. Beat at medium speed for 2½ minutes. Scrape bowl and beaters. Add milk in three parts, beating at low speed about 1 minute after each addition or until smooth.

Pour into prepared pan and bake immediately 18 to 20 minutes. Turn out on rack, remove paper. Place rack over sheet of cake and turn over again. Cool top side up.

Mix and bake a second sheet of cake as directed above. Cool.

Prepare 1 recipe of Custard Cream Filling or Lemon Filling (see Index). Cut cakes down the center the short way, making two rectangles from each. Spread one third of the filling on one piece of cake. Cover with second piece of cake. Continue until four sheets of cake are stacked with three layers of filling between them. Trim edges of cake evenly on all four sides. Cut into four lengthwise strips. Frost top and sides of each strip with Buttercream Frosting No. 1 (see Index). Cover sides with finely chopped nuts or shaved semi-sweet chocolate. Cut each strip into four pieces. Place pieces in fluted paper cups or on serving plate. Border each piece with Buttercream pressed through a No. 16 tube. Decorate with small flowers or outline small sections and fill with jelly. Yield: 3½ cups batter; 16 pieces.

Napoleons

Preheat oven to 425° F.
Two 12" x 15" cookie sheets;
  do not grease.

Puff Paste

1 cup butter	½ cup ice water
1¾ cups sifted, all-purpose flour	

Allow ⅔ cup of butter to warm to room temperature before starting to mix pastry. Keep remaining ⅓ cup of butter refrigerated until needed. To mix, cut the cold butter into the flour with a pastry blender until the mixture resembles coarse meal. Add enough ice water to hold ingredients together. Roll dough out on a floured board to a ten-inch square about ¼" thick. Divide the ⅔ cup of soft butter into fourths. Spread ¼ of butter over ⅔ of the square of dough. Fold unbuttered ⅓ over to center of buttered portion; fold remaining ⅓ over top. The dough should now be folded into thirds with butter between each layer. Roll again; repeat procedure. Chill dough 30 minutes. Repeat procedure twice more. Chill dough 30 to 45 minutes.

Remove chilled dough from refrigerator, divide in half, return one piece to the refrigerator. Roll the other piece of dough on an ungreased cookie sheet to a rectangle about 10"x12"x⅛". (If the cookie sheet has four sides, roll the dough on the bottom instead.) Prick the entire surface of the rolled dough with a fork. Chill on cookie sheet in refrigerator for 30 minutes before baking. Bake for 10 to 15 minutes or until lightly browned. Remove from oven and cool on cookie sheet placed on rack. Repeat with second piece of dough; cool.

When pastry is cool, straighten edges, using a ruler to form a rectangle about 9"x11" (the pastry sheet will have shrunk somewhat in baking). Cut the pastry down the center lengthwise, making two strips of equal size. Repeat with second piece of cooled pastry.

Filling and Decoration

1 recipe Custard Cream Filling   ¼ cup semi-sweet chocolate bits
   (see Index)   1 teaspoon butter
¼ recipe Cookie Glaze
   (see Index)

While the dough is chilling, make Custard Cream Filling; let cool. To assemble Napoleons, place 1 strip of pastry, bottom side down, on a clean cookie sheet. Spread with ⅓ of cooled Custard Cream Filling. Top with another strip of pastry. Continue in this manner until you have piled four strips of pastry with Filling between them. Place the last strip *bottom side up* for a smoother surface on which to spread the Glaze. Refrigerate pastry about 1 hour to set the filling.

Meanwhile, make up one-quarter recipe Cookie Glaze. Spread glaze quickly over pastry; allow to set. Melt ¼ cup semi-sweet chocolate bits over warm water; stir 1 teaspoon of butter into melted chocolate until blended. Pour melted chocolate into a small paper or parchment cone. Cut tip to about the size of a No. 6 tube. Pipe diagonal lines about ½" apart over glaze. Allow chocolate to set a little before cutting pastry into 6 pieces about 1¾"x4½". Use a very sharp knife and a sawing motion to avoid crushing the pastry. It will also be helpful to clean the knife blade after each piece is cut. Place on serving plate or in individual fluted paper cups. Refrigerate until serving time. Yield: 6 Napoleons each 1¾"x4½".

DECORATING NOTE: The simple chocolate icing is traditional on Napoleons but a web design traced in chocolate is a professional touch. Sweetened, firmly whipped cream may be substituted for the Custard Cream Filling.

French Tarts

Preheat oven to 425° F.
Bake in twelve 3" fluted tart pans
  or twenty-four 3¼" x 1¾" oval tartlette pans;
    set the pans on a 12" x 15" cookie sheet for easy handling.

2½ cups sifted, all-purpose flour	½ cup butter, cold
6 tablespoons sugar	1 egg
1 teaspoon baking powder	2 tablespoons ice water

Sift flour, sugar and baking powder together 3 times. Add butter and cut in with pastry blender until the mixture resembles coarse meal. Stir in egg and enough ice water to make a firm dough. Wrap dough in waxed paper and chill for 1 hour.

Place about 2 tablespoons of dough in each tart pan. With the thumbs of both hands, press the dough evenly over the bottom and sides of each pan. Prick dough all over with a fork. Set tarts on a cookie sheet and bake for 10 minutes or until browned. Turn each pan over on the cookie sheet and tap gently to release tart shells. If any of the shells are not brown enough at the bottom and sides, leave them in this position on the cookie sheet and return to the oven for about 4 minutes longer. Cool top side up on a rack.

(If you are using small tart pans, press only 1 tablespoon of dough into each. Bake 12 at a time and keep remaining dough refrigerated until the first 12 tarts are baked.)

Fill cooled tart shells with berries or small pieces of fruit. Cover with Fruit Glaze (see Index). Garnish with whipped cream if desired.

VARIATION: Fill cooled tart shells with Vanilla, Chocolate or Coffee Custard Cream Filling (see Index). Whip ½ pint heavy cream until stiff. Attach pastry tube No. 6 (star tube) to decorating bag or paper cone. Fill with whipped cream. Pipe designs as desired. Sprinkle with grated semi-sweet chocolate or chopped nuts.

Petits Fours

Preheat oven to 350° F.
Grease bottom and line with paper:
One 17" x 11½" x 1" pan
    or two 9" x 13" x 2" pans.

1 recipe Basic Sponge Cake,   ¼ cup cake flour
  Genoise, or Enriched Yellow Cake   1 recipe Fondant Icing (see Index)

Bake the cake a few hours or a day in advance so you can freeze it to make cutting easier. Follow the basic cake recipe but add ¼ cup sifted cake flour for a more compact texture. Bake as directed in prepared pan(s). Spread a sheet of wax paper or release paper (see Sources of Supply) over the cake rack, invert pan(s) on cake rack and peel off paper liner(s). Let cake(s) cool on paper-covered rack. Trim crusts from four sides of cake or cakes. Cut large cake into two pieces; leave smaller cakes whole. Place the cakes on cardboards covered with wax paper, and wrap each piece in freezer paper or in plastic bag. Freeze until firm. (Cake can be kept in freezer for several weeks.)

When ready to decorate, prepare Easy Fondant Icing (see Index). Remove one cake from the freezer, cut with petits fours cutters or a sharp knife (see chart). Dip the knife blade into hot water often to make clean cuts.

Arrange pieces of cake on a cake rack placed over a clean cookie sheet. Pour or spoon lukewarm Fondant over cake pieces, being careful to cover completely. Let set 5 minutes. If coating appears too thin, scrape Fondant which has dripped onto cookie sheet back into saucepan. Heat over very low heat to 100° F, and spoon over cakes again. Add a teaspoon of hot water if Fondant becomes too thick. Yield: About 36 Petits Fours from each cake.

When Fondant has set completely, remove petits fours from rack.

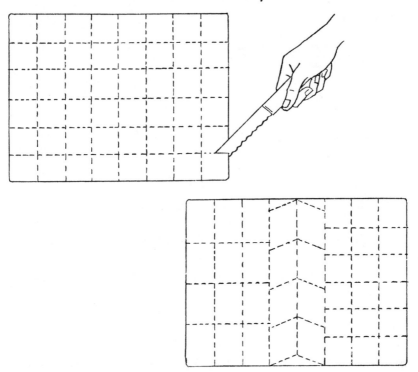

Fig. 4. Chart for cutting Petits Fours. a 48 squares; b 38 squares, rectangles and diamonds.

Trim away any droplets of Fondant from the bottom edges. Place in individual fluted cups or on a pretty serving plate. Decorate tops with dainty designs shown in photo using either Decorator or Royal Icing. I prefer Royal Icing because it's firmer and won't break as easily when dried.

NOTE: If you prefer to dip cakes into the Fondant, cut them as described above, then return them to the freezer. Remove only 6 or 8 pieces at a time. Hold each piece in the fingertips and dip into the icing, top side down. Allow only the top and sides of the pieces to become coated with icing. Turn the piece over and place on rack, uncoated side down. (The fingerprints will be covered by the settling fondant.) If the pieces of cake are frozen solidly you will have no trouble with crumbs falling into the icing. I prefer to dip the pieces because better coverage is possible, but it is the slower way.

Summer Coating (see Index) is also a good icing for Petits Fours.

Cream Puffs

Preheat oven to 425° F.
One 12" x 15" cookie sheet;
    do not grease.

1 cup water	1 cup sifted, all-purpose flour
⅛ teaspoon salt	½ teaspoon baking powder
½ cup shortening	3 eggs

Combine water, salt, and shortening in medium-size saucepan. Place over high heat till water boils and shortening is melted. Reduce heat to low. Add flour all at once and stir constantly till mixture leaves the sides of the pan and forms a ball. Remove pan from heat. Sprinkle baking powder over surface of paste. Add eggs one at a time, beating well after each addition. If you wish to use electric mixer, transfer ball of paste to mixer bowl when it is removed from the stove and proceed as above.

Drop Cream Puffs 2-3 inches apart on ungreased cookie sheet, using a pastry bag with star tube No. 6 or plain tube No. 9. Bake at 425° for 20-25 minutes, then reduce heat to 350° and bake 15 minutes longer. Test Puffs by placing one on a wire rack. If it holds its shape after 1 minute, it is done; if it softens and loses shape, continue baking for 5 minutes more. Let Puffs cool. When cold, make a slit in each or remove top portions with a sharp knife. Fill with whipped cream, ice cream or Custard Cream Filling (see Index), using pastry tube No. 6 or a spoon. Yield: 16 large or 48 small Cream Puffs.

Cream Puff Swans

Preheat oven to 400° F.
Two 12" x 15" cookie sheets;
    do not grease.

Follow recipe for Cream Puffs. Attach a No. 9 pastry tube (plain tube) to a 14" or 16" pastry bag. Pipe 14 question-mark shaped pieces about 3" long on one cookie sheet (these will be used as heads and necks of the swans). Bake for 15 minutes or until lightly browned. Cool by placing cookie sheet on rack.

Raise temperature of the oven to 425° F. On second cookie sheet pipe oval mounds of dough about 2" long, spacing them about 3" apart. Bake for 20 minutes then reduce oven temperature to 350° and bake until lightly browned, about 15 minutes longer. Carefully remove from cookie sheet and place on rack to cool.

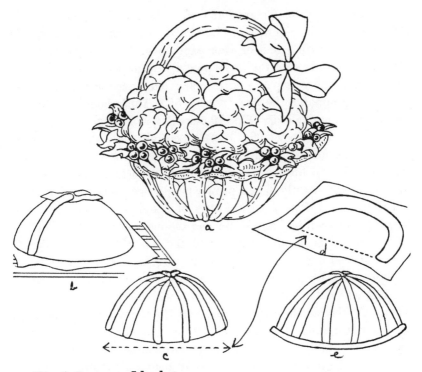

Fig. 5. Cream puff basket.

To assemble, cut upper third from each oval, being careful not to break the pieces. Cut a hole in the tip of each oval large enough for the end of the neck. Fill ovals with Custard Cream, ice cream, or sweetened whipped cream. Carefully insert the ends of the necks into the holes in the bodies, pressing slightly to keep them in an upright position. Cut the ovals removed from the tops in half lengthwise and insert into filling for wings. Dust lightly with confectioners' sugar before serving. If desired, pipe a tiny dot of a brown frosting or piping gel on each side of the heads for eyes. Refrigerate until serving time. If filled with ice cream, store in the freezer. Yield: 12-14 Swans.

Cream Puff Basket

Preheat oven to 375° F.
Generously grease the *outside* of a
   3- or 4-cup metal or ovenproof
   glass bowl. Have ready a 12" x 15"
   ungreased cookie sheet.

Follow recipe for Cream Puffs. Fit tube No. 47st into a 14" or 16" pastry bag; fill with dough. Place bowl on wax paper-covered cake rack. Press a small circle of wax paper over the top of the bowl. Starting at the center of the bowl, pipe a strip of dough over the bowl and down to the wax paper on the rack. Turn rack around and pipe second strip opposite the first (see fig. 5*b*). Tube should be held flat side up when piping strips. Pipe 10 more strips of dough, spacing them evenly around the bowl (fig. *c*). Connect all the ends of the strips by piping a continuous strip of dough around the bowl where it meets the rack (fig. *e*). Moisten the tip of a small spatula with water; use to connect and slightly flatten point where strips come together at the top of the bowl. Pipe a curved strip of dough on cookie sheet (for handle), as shown in figure *d*. Be sure the measurement between both ends is the same as the diameter of the top of the bowl (fig. *d*). Pipe a second handle in case of breakage. The two may also be put together with Royal Icing for a nice round handle. Refrigerate the handles while the basket is baking; it will take about 50 minutes. Then bake the handle about 30 minutes. The times can vary, however, so watch carefully. Both the basket and handle should be nicely browned and puffy before they are removed from the oven.

Allow the basket to cool completely before attempting to remove from bowl. Carefully peel away the wax paper. Allow handle to cool on cookie sheet 5 minutes, then remove to rack to cool completely.

Attach handle to basket with toothpicks and a dab of Royal Icing. Tie a ribbon bow to handle.

Decorate edges of basket with Royal Icing, using any seasonal design.

Make Cream Puffs from remaining dough as directed in recipe. Store filled Puffs in refrigerator and arrange in basket shortly before serving time.

Eclairs

Preheat oven to 425° F.
One 12" x 15" cookie sheet;
　do not grease.

Follow recipe for Cream Puffs. Press strips of dough 1"x3½" long from pastry bag, using star tube No. 8 or plain tube No. 9. Bake as for Cream Puffs.

When cool, make a tiny hole in one end or split lengthwise. Fill with Custard Cream (see Index) using a teaspoon, or pipe in with pastry bag and plain tube No. 6. Cover tops with Chocolate Glaze (see Index) or sprinkle with confectioners' sugar. Yield: 14 Eclairs.

Meringue Shells

Preheat oven to 250° F.
Cover with brown wrapping paper:
One 12" x 15" cookie sheet;
    do not grease paper.

3 egg whites (at room temperature)	¼ teaspoon cream of tartar
½ teaspoon salt	¾ cup superfine granulated sugar

Trace eight 2½" circles on the brown paper covering the cookie sheet, spacing them 1½" apart. Combine egg whites, salt, and cream of tartar in bowl of electric mixer. Beat at medium speed until mixture stands in soft peaks. Add sugar 1 tablespoon at a time beating after each addition. Continue to beat for 6 to 8 minutes longer or until mixture is very stiff and sugar is completely dissolved.

Attach pastry tube No. 6 (star tube) to a 14" or 16" pastry bag and fill with Meringue. Starting at the center of each circle, pipe a flat disc in a circular motion, covering the circle. Pipe a rim around the outer edge of each disc. Bake for 35 minutes, turn off the heat and keep the Meringues in the oven with the door closed until they have cooled completely.

Remove the shells from the paper carefully using a spatula or a pancake turner. Place on large serving plate or individual plates. Before serving fill with ice cream, chilled chocolate or lemon pudding, berries or fruit. Garnish with whipped cream if desired. Yield: 8 shells.

DECORATING NOTE: Meringues may be piped into heart, shamrock, bell or oval shapes. For uniformity trace the outlines on the paper before shaping. If color is desired dissolve a small amount of paste color in the unbeaten egg whites. Finely chopped nuts may be sprinkled on the meringues before baking for further variety. For crisper, slightly browned meringues bake for 55 minutes before turning oven off. Proceed as directed above.

Jelly Roll

Preheat oven to 350° F.
Grease and line with wax paper
    or release paper (see Sources of Supply):
One 10" x 15" jelly roll pan.

5 eggs, separated
1 teaspoon vanilla extract
¾ cup sugar
¾ cup sifted cake flour
½ teaspoon baking powder

¼ teaspoon salt
Confectioners' sugar
1¼ cups Buttercream Frosting No. 1
    (see Index)
1 eight-ounce jar tart or sweet jelly

Combine egg yolks and vanilla in large bowl of electric mixer. Beat at medium speed until well blended. Add granulated sugar to egg yolks and beat at medium speed 5 to 8 minutes or until mixture is thick and lemon colored. In another large bowl beat egg whites stiff but not dry. Fold whites gently into yolk mixture. Sift flour, baking powder and salt together. Fold dry ingredients into egg mixture. Carefully spread batter into prepared pan. Bake immediately about 15 minutes or until cake tester comes out clean when inserted into cake.

Sift a coat of confectioners' sugar over a clean linen dish towel which has been spread on a smooth work surface. Turn the cake out on the sugar-dusted towel. Carefully remove the waxed paper. Trim crusts from four sides of the cake. Roll cake, starting at the short edge, using the towel to help you lift it. Wrap the towel around the rolled cake. Cool on a cake rack with the loose edge of the roll down and slightly underneath it.

Filling and Decoration

1¼ cups Buttercream Frosting No. 1   1 8-ounce jar tart or sweet jelly
    (see Index)

When cool, unroll cake carefully. Spread with Buttercream Frosting No. 1, then jelly. Reroll cake tightly. Dust with confectioners' sugar. Yield: 10 servings.

DECORATING NOTE: This sponge cake roll may be baked in two 8" round layer pans, and filled with Lemon Filling frosted with Lemon Icing (see Index).

Chocolate Nut Torte

Preheat oven to 350° F.
Grease bottoms and line with paper:
 grease wax paper generously:
Two 8" round pans.

6 eggs, separated	¾ cup sifted cake flour
1½ cups sifted confectioners' sugar	1 teaspoon baking powder

Beat egg yolks at medium speed until thick and lemon colored. Add confectioners' sugar and continue to beat until blended. Sift flour and baking powder together and fold into egg yolks and sugar. Beat egg whites until stiff and fold into yolk mixture. Pour into prepared pans and bake 15 to 20 minutes or until cake tester comes out clean when inserted into the center. Turn out of pans immediately and remove paper. Turn top side up on racks and cool thoroughly.

While cakes are cooling make 1 recipe Chocolate Buttercream (see Index) and chop 2 cups of walnuts or pecans for garnish.

When cake layers have cooled split each lengthwise making 2 thin layers from each. Place first layer on serving plate cut side up. Spread with a ½" thick layer of buttercream and sprinkle with about ⅓ of the nuts. Top with second layer of cake. Repeat until 4 layers of cake are stacked with buttercream and nuts between them. Use bottom half of second layer, crust side up, as the top for a smoother frosting surface. Spread top with buttercream but *do not* sprinkle with nuts. Attach a No. 30 tube to a decorating bag or paper cone, fill with Chocolate Buttercream and pipe a criss-cross lattice design and a shell border on the top layer of the Torte. Yield: 3½ cups batter; 16-20 servings.

NOTE: Cover and refrigerate any leftover buttercream for future use. Allow to come to room temperature first, then rebeat to restore fluffy consistency before using.

Ice Cream Cake

Two 8" or 9" round layer cakes	1 pint heavy cream
½ gallon brick ice cream	1 package whipped topping mix

Bake the layers following the recipe for yellow, chocolate or marble cake (see Index). If the layers are more than 1" thick, slice a bit of cake from each, and use scraps in puddings or for the children.

Use any flavor of ice cream that will compliment the flavor of the cake.

Prepare whipped topping mix as directed on package except add the heavy cream when the topping forms soft peaks. Continue to beat until the mixture is stiff. The whipped topping mix acts as a stabilizer for the heavy cream, so you can enjoy the flavor of the cream and the convenience of a stabilized topping.

Cover a corrugated cardboard cake circle 12″ in diameter with aluminum foil or a doily. If a doily is used, secure it to the cardboard with a dab of piping gel or cream.

Center the first cake layer on the board, top side up. Spread with a thin coat of cream. Open the ice cream carton on all sides so as to expose all but the bottom of the brick. Cut the brick into lengthwise slices 1″ thick. Place two slices side by side on top of the cake layer. Trim the ice cream level with the edge of the cake all around. If necessary, use more ice cream to cover any exposed cake. (Return any leftover ice cream to the freezer. If the carton cannot be used again, place ice cream in a plastic container with a cover on it.) Spread the top of the ice cream layer with a thin coat of whipped cream. Top with other cake layer bottom side up for a smoother surface. Spread entire cake with whipped cream, reserving some to pipe on a top and a bottom border if cake is to be decorated. If ice cream becomes too soft during this, place cake in the freezer to firm up, then proceed as described above.

Place in cake box (see Sources of Supply), seal and place in freezer till serving time. If a box is not available, place cake unwrapped in freezer until firm, then place in plastic bag or wrap in freezer wrap. Yield: 16 servings.

Cookies

Imagine, no more drop cookies that look like maps of South America! Doughs that are normally dropped from the tip of a spoon can be pressed from a bag to produce perfectly round cookies. Even if you have always pressed cookies from a metal cylinder with a plunger or a crank, you will be pleased by the ease and speed with which cookies can be formed using a pastry bag and tubes. The bag responds to your touch so much faster, enabling you to produce cookies of uniform shape and size.

Be sure the cookie dough is at the proper consistency. Several factors are involved here but the most important ones are the eggs and the flour. Eggs vary in size and so will the amount of flour they can absorb; therefore, it may be necessary to add more or less flour than the recipe specifies. After a while, experience will tell you when the dough is just right, but until then do this:

1. Do not add all the flour called for (unless the dough appears very soft—this could occur when very large eggs are used). Press out a small amount of dough using your decorating bag and tube. You should not have to exert a great deal of pressure; the shape of the cookie should be sharp because some grooves, etc. are normally lost during baking. Add more flour if it seems necessary.

Fig. 6. Designs for painting cookies, and decorating cookie Christmas-tree ornaments.

2. If the cookies are for a special occasion, or if you want to be absolutely sure the dough is perfect, bake the first few you press out. This will take only a few minutes and it could save you from having a tray or two of cookies you are not happy with. If the baked cookies have held their shape, press out the remaining dough; otherwise adjust the consistency still further.

Before you have baked many batches of cookies, you will know when the dough is right just from the feel of it.

TO PRESS BAR-TYPE COOKIES OR SHELL-SHAPED ONES, hold the bag at about a 60-degree angle to the cookie sheet. For most other shapes, hold it straight up and down and slightly above the cookie sheet. Starting from this postiion, the bag may also be given a slight twist to make a cookie similar to a drop flower in shape.

YOUR FAVORITE CUT-OUT COOKIE may be decorated using Royal Icing. Very pretty effects may be achieved by first spreading some cookies with Cookie Glaze in a pastel shade and then accenting them with touches of Royal Icing.

Cookie dough may be stored in the refrigerator for about two weeks. Butter cookies are difficult to press out if the dough is cold, so allow it to return to room temperature before using.

Party Cookies

Preheat oven to 400° F.
Grease cookie sheet lightly.

2 cups sifted all-purpose flour	½ cup soft butter or margarine
1 cup sugar	1 egg, unbeaten
¼ teaspoon salt	2 tablespoons milk
½ teaspoon baking powder	1 teaspoon vanilla extract

Sift together flour, sugar, salt and baking powder. Add butter or margarine and cut in with pastry blender until mixture resembles coarse crumbs. Stir in egg, milk and vanilla. Knead dough lightly to blend ingredients and form into a ball. Wrap in wax paper or plastic wrap and chill 4 hours or longer so dough will handle easily.

Divide chilled dough into 4 parts. Roll each on a floured pastry cloth or board to slightly less than ¼" thickness. Cut with floured cookie cutters and place 1 to 1½" apart on cookie sheet. Bake 6 to 9 minutes.

CAUTION NOTE: The temperature of the dough after it is chilled will influence baking time. Before removing all the cookies from the oven, break one open to check the inside for doneness. If the cookie still appears doughy inside, bake for another minute or two. Remove from cookie sheet and cool on racks. Spread with Cookie Glaze and decorate with tiny colored candies or Royal Icing (see Index). Yield: About 70 cookies.

Variation

Substitute orange or lemon extract for the vanilla. Ice with orange or yellow colored Cookie Glaze (see Index) which has been flavored the same as the cookie dough.

Cookie Christmas-Tree Ornaments

After Party Cookies have baked 5 minutes, punch a hole in the upper part of each, about ¼″ from the edge, using a skewer or similar instrument. Return to oven to complete baking. When cool loop a ribbon or string through the holes for hanging on the tree.

Vanilla Cookies

Preheat oven to 350° F.
Ungreased cookie sheet.

1 cup vegetable shortening (part butter may be used but dough will be soft and may require extra flour for easier handling)	6 cups sifted all-purpose flour
	1 teaspoon baking soda
	1 teaspoon salt
	2 teaspoons vanilla extract
2 cups sugar	1 cup commercial sour cream

Cream shortening and sugar until fluffy. Sift together dry ingredients; add to shortening with vanilla, and sour cream. Blend dough thoroughly, cover and chill several hours or overnight. Roll chilled dough on lightly floured board to ⅛″ thickness. Cut into fancy shapes or use plain round cutter about 3″ in diameter. Bake 10 to 15 minutes. Watch carefully the last few minutes to avoid overbrowning. Remove from cookie sheet and cool on racks. Yield: About 7 dozen cookies.

DECORATING NOTE: These cookies may be painted with egg yolk paint before baking or painted and decorated with Cookie Glaze and Royal Icing (see Index) after baking.

Butter Cookies

Preheat oven to 400° F.
Ungreased cookie sheet.

1 cup butter	1 teaspoon vanilla extract
¾ cup sugar	2¼ cups sifted all-purpose flour
1 egg	½ teaspoon baking powder

Cream butter, sugar, and egg until fluffy. Add extract. Sift flour and baking powder together and stir into creamed mixture. Fill pastry bag or cookie press and form cookies on ungreased cookie sheet. Bake for 8 to 10 minutes, or until lightly browned at edges. Remove from cookie sheet and cool on racks. Yield: About 5 dozen cookies.

DECORATING NOTE: Cookies may be decorated before baking with chocolate sprinkles, tiny colored nonpareils, bits of maraschino or candied cherries, etc. If nuts or chocolate chips are added to batter, press out with a round tube.

BAR COOKIES may be pressed out in strips across the cookie sheet and cut into uniform-size pieces immediately after they are removed from the oven. They may be served plain, or sandwiched with melted chocolate. The ends of the sandwiches may be dipped first in melted chocolate, then into chopped nuts or chocolate sprinkles.

CINNAMON COOKIES: Knead 1 tablespoon of cinnamon into half the finished dough. Press out with star tube and center each with a piece of a walnut or pecan. Use vanilla as flavoring when you are planning to add cinnamon to part of the dough.

Chocolate Butter Cookies

Preheat oven to 375° F.
Ungreased cookie sheet.

¾ cup butter or margarine	1½ cups sifted all purpose flour
1 cup sugar	½ cup cocoa
1 egg, unbeaten	2 tablespoons cream or undiluted
1½ teaspoons vanilla extract	evaporated milk

Cream butter, sugar, egg and vanilla thoroughly. Sift flour and cocoa together and add alternately with cream. Fill a pastry bag or cookie press and form cookies on ungreased cookie sheet. Press a piece of nutmeat or maraschino cherry into the center of each. Bake for 8 to 10 minutes. Remove from cookie sheet and cool on racks. Yield: About 5 dozen cookies.

Frosty Nut Crescents

Preheat oven to 375° F.
Ungreased cookie sheet.

1 cup butter or margarine,
    room temperature
¼ cup confectioners' sugar
1½ teaspoons water
2 teaspoons vanilla extract

2 cups unsifted all-purpose flour
1 cup finely chopped nuts (pecans,
    walnuts, or almonds)
Additional confectioners' sugar
    to roll cookies in

Cream butter and sugar. Add remaining ingredients and mix till well blended. Roll small portions of dough into ropes about ½" thick on lightly floured board. Cut into 1" pieces, lay on ungreased cookie sheet and pull ends down, forming small crescents. Bake for about 15 minutes. Roll warm cookies in confectioners' sugar. Roll in sugar a second time when thoroughly cooled. Yield: About 6 dozen cookies.

"Strawberry" Cookies (Unbaked)

1 pound finely ground coconut
¼ pound ground nuts (blanched
    almonds, pecans, or walnuts)
2 tablespoons sugar

2 packages strawberry-flavored
    gelatin (reserve ½ package)
1 can (14- or 15-ounce) sweetened
    condensed milk

Mix all ingredients except the reserved gelatin. Shape a small amount of the mixture at a time into the shape of a strawberry. Roll each "strawberry" in a mixture of the reserved ½ cup of gelatin and 4 tablespoons of red sugar (see Note). Add three small Royal Icing leaves to the top of each or place a Marzipan strawberry hull (see Sources of Supply) into the top of each.

NOTE: To color the sugar, add a bit of red color to it and rub between the fingertips or purchase pre-colored sugar available in the baking sections of Food Markets.

Cookie Glaze

3 cups sifted confectioners' sugar
¼ cup warm water

1 tablespoon white corn syrup
¼ teaspoon flavoring

Mix sugar, water, corn syrup and flavoring until well blended and smooth. Spread quickly over cookies and allow to dry thoroughly before decorating with Royal Icing. If glaze is too thick to spread easily add and stir in a few drops of hot water. Yield: ¾ of a cup or enough to cover about 36 3″ cookies.

Chocolate Cookie Glaze

Following recipe for Cookie Glaze sifting ¼ cup of cocoa with the confectioners' sugar. Increase water to 5 tablespoons and use vanilla extract as flavoring. Yield: About 1 cup or enough to cover 12 to 15 eclairs.

NOTE: The flavor of these glazes may be improved by heating slightly before using.

Egg Yolk Cookie Paint

2 egg yolks　　　　　　　　　Coloring
2 teaspoons milk

Mix together egg yolks and milk. Divide mixture into as many portions as needed and tint with food colors. Using a clean brush for each color, apply mixture to paint design on cookies before baking.

DECORATING NOTE: The cookies will have brightly colored shiny designs on them when they come from the oven. The illustrations show only a few of the designs possible. Cookie painting can be done by every member of the family, including the youngest, on any rolled cookie.

Chapter 3

FROSTINGS AND FILLINGS
(Techniques and Recipes)

Frosting (or icing, I use the words interchangeably) enhances the flavor of the cake of course, and helps keep it fresh by sealing out air.

Cover cake with a thin coat of frosting as soon as it is cool; for maximum freshness, let it stand at least four hours or overnight before you apply the finish coat.

All the frosting recipes in this book are delicious but cakes that are to be decorated need easy-to-spread frostings that will not crust over (the way icings made up largely of confectioners' sugar will do). Because they stay creamy, making it possible for even a beginner to achieve a smooth surface, I recommend these frostings for cakes to be decorated: Buttercream Frosting No. 1, White Whipped Buttercream No. 2, Chocolate Buttercream and Creamy Frosting.

Frosting the Cake

1. Be sure cake is cool and level. Trim away any bumps or uneven places with a serrated knife. (Use the trimmed pieces as a dessert topping.) Place leveled cake, top side down, on the prepared base. (The bottom is a better surface to frost over.) Brush away any loose crumbs with a soft brush.

2. Place the cake and its base on a turntable or lazy susan.

3. If you have time, apply a thin coat of icing and allow it to set a few hours or overnight; this will be a great help in holding the crumbs to the surface so they will not get into the finished frosting.

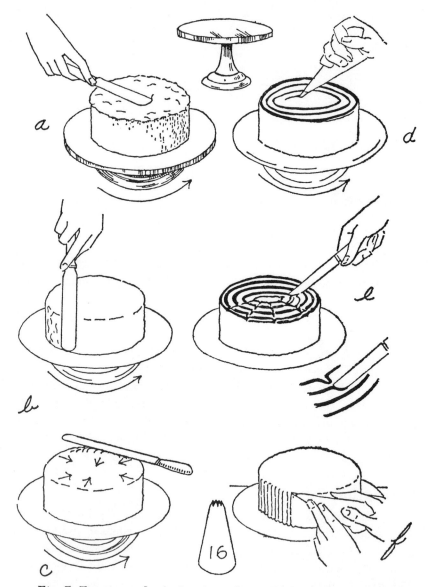

Fig. 7. Frosting cake (a, b, c); spider web design (d, e); and striating sides (f).

4. If time does not permit using this method, apply icing to the cake surface with long strokes of a flexible icing spatula. Use plenty of icing; this will keep you from pulling up crumbs. The excess will be removed when the icing is smoothed.

5. Apply frosting to the sides of the cake in the same way. Smooth the top of the cake with the flat of the spatula, the tip held just past the center of the cake (figure 7a). With the spatula in this position, revolve the turntable once or twice. Return to the bowl the excess icing picked up by spatula. At this point, the cake top should be completely covered, though not perfectly smooth.

6. Next hold the blade of the spatula against the side of the cake, handle straight up (figure 7b). Revolve turntable while holding the spatula in this position. It may be necessary to make two or more revolutions of the turntable before the icing is completely smooth. If cake shows through, cover the spot with icing. Place spatula against it and turn the turntable again to smooth the spot. With the edge of the spatula, draw excess icing from the top edge toward the center (figure 7c). Hold the spatula so that only one edge touches the cake surface.

Spider web design and striating sides

For spider web design, pipe circles of chocolate frosting over cake covered with a light color icing (7d). Gently draw the end of spatula through circles, starting at center each time (7e).

If the sides of the cake are to be striated, apply only a thin coat of icing to the sides with a spatula. (Frost the cake top as usual.) Attach a No. 16 tube to a bag filled with frosting. Striate the sides with an up-and-down motion of the tube, being careful to come up to the same level at the top edge each time (figure 7f). This method of finishing the sides of a cake is especially useful when the cake crust is rather dark, making it difficult to cover with icing applied in the usual way.

Add the top border after striated sides are completed. The bottom edge may be bordered at this time or left plain.

Storing frosted cake

If cakes frosted with buttercream are used within 24 hours there is hardly any need to refrigerate them unless the house is very warm. If they are refrigerated, store them covered or boxed as buttercream tends to absorb odors from other foods. Remove from the refrigerator at least 1½ hours before serving. The delicate flavor of buttercream can be lost completely if it is too cold.

Storing frosting

Unless otherwise noted, the frostings included in this section will keep well if refrigerated in a tightly covered container. If they contain butter and milk, they can be stored for two or three weeks; otherwise they will last for 5 or 6 months. To use, allow frosting to warm to room temperature before beating again to restore its fluffy consistency.

If frosting looks curdled

If you attempt to beat buttercream before it has warmed sufficiently, the butter will separate from the other ingredients and it will look curdled. The flavor will be unchanged but it will not spread or pipe nicely. If this occurs there are two courses open to you. 1) You can let the frosting stand until it is warmer, then rebeat it. 2) Or melt about 2 tablespoons of butter over very low heat. Start beating the frosting and pour the melted butter over it in a very thin stream. Continue to beat until the frosting is fluffy and no longer looks curdled. Use 2 tablespoons of butter for about 1½ cups of frosting but this amount can vary depending on how cold the frosting is. More melted butter may be added if necessary.

About amounts of frostings

You may notice that the amount of frosting called for in our decorated cakes is generous, and there are several reasons why this is so. First and perhaps most important, it should never be necessary to stretch frosting; to do so makes a really smooth surface virtually impossible to achieve. A border is used on most decorated cakes and these require extra frosting. Then too it is difficult to work with less than ¾ cup frosting in a decorating bag, although a great many decorations do not require that much. Smaller amounts may be placed in a small parchment cone, but here too it would be impossible to fill the bag with just the exact amount needed because some frosting always clings to the sides. This frosting need not be wasted, however; it can be scraped back into its container and refrigerated for future use. When you need just a minute quantity (for a small dot or one tiny drop flower) place the frosting directly into the tube. Then, with tube between thumb and third finger press out with the tip of the second finger. This takes a little practice so please don't try it on an important cake till you get the knack of it.

All things considered, we have allowed for the things mentioned above, plus a little extra for samples given to the children, and for tastes taken by the decorator.

1 recipe of Buttercream No. 1, Chocolate Buttercream, Creamy Frosting or Chocolate Fudge Frosting will be sufficient to:

> Fill, frost and border a 9" round 2-layer cake.
> Frost and border a 10" round 2-layer cake.
> Frost and border a 10" square sheet cake.
> Frost and border an 8"x14" sheet cake.

1½ recipes of the above frostings will be required to (generously) frost and border a 12" square sheet cake.

2 recipes of the above frostings will be required to frost and border a 12"x17½" sheet cake.

1 recipe of White Whipped Buttercream will be sufficient for the following (amounts are generous):

> Fill, frost and border a 12" round 2-layer cake.
> Fill, frost and border a 10" 2-layer cake.
> Frost and border a 10" square sheet cake.
> Frost and border an 8"x14" sheet cake.
> Frost and border a 12" square sheet cake.

1½ recipes of White Whipped Frosting will be required to frost and border a 12"x17½" sheet cake.

Coloring the Frosting

Food colors come in three forms: liquid, powder and paste.

LIQUID COLORS available in supermarkets are unsatisfactory. A true red or any deep shade cannot be achieved because you need so much liquid that the icing becomes too thin and watery. Professional liquid colors (see Sources of Supply) available through bakers' supply houses, while better than those in the food stores, still leave much to be desired.

POWDERED COLORS work well. Some bakers import them from Europe but they are not generally available to homemakers.

PASTE COLORS are best for all coloring needs. They are a bit more expensive than the liquids but considering the smaller amount you'll need, and the better results you'll obtain, you will find the pastes more economical in the end.

Mixing colors

I prefer not to mix two or more colors of icing together to obtain a different color because the results are seldom satisfactory. The better liquid and paste colors are available in a wide range of colors. In some cases there are two strengths of one color, one for regular shades and the other for very deep shades. Paste colors are available in a 10-color set of 1-ounce jars, and in an 8-color set of ½-ounce jars; they also come individually. Commercial liquid colors come in 4-ounce or 8-ounce bottles.

How to mix color into frosting

Frosting colors are frequently limited to pastels, but there are times when only a bright color will do. Children's cakes, for example, are often bright as are the festive reds and greens on Christmas cakes. If you use black, it should be really black, not grayish.

Add the color to only a small portion of the white frosting and blend carefully, being certain there are no streaks. Gradually add the colored to the white frosting until you get the desired shade. If, when all the colored frosting has been added, the shade is still not deep enough, repeat the procedure. Colors tend to deepen after the frosting stands awhile, so check after 15-20 minutes if you want an exact tone. All the colors dissolve instantly.

Use small stainless steel or crockery bowls for mixing the frosting and colors.

How much paste color to use

Opposite each color I list the suggested quantity to be used for one cup of decorating frosting. However, such factors as the moisture content of the frosting influence the amount needed. Also, you require less paste for coloring piping gel than for coloring frosting. So use the quantities listed as a general guide only.

"Toothpick" quantity means the amount of color that will cling to the tip of a toothpick.

You will find listed below all the colors available and the suggested amounts to use. Those marked with an asterisk are the ones which I used consistently in decorating the cakes shown in the color photographs.

SCARLET RED: Use 2 to 3 teaspoons; let frosting stand 20 minutes for full brilliance.

CHRISTMAS RED: Brighter than Scarlet Red. Use 2 to 3 teaspoons; let frosting stand 20 minutes for full brilliance.

RED-RED: Same as Christmas Red but double strength. Use 1 teaspoon; let frosting stand 20 minutes for full brilliance.

*VALENTINE RED: Brightest of all reds; use 2 teaspoons. Let frosting stand 20 minutes for full brilliance.

ROYAL RED: A little darker than Scarlet Red; use 2 to 3 teaspoons. Let frosting stand 20 minutes for full brilliance.

CRIMSON RED: Darkest of all reds. Use 2 to 3 teaspoons. Let frosting stand 20 minutes for full brilliance.

*ROSE PINK: Pastels—"toothpick" quantity.

*SKY BLUE: Pastels—"toothpick" quantity. Deep tones—⅛ teaspoon.

MARINE BLUE: Much darker than Sky Blue. Deep tones only—¼ to ½ teaspoon.

MINT GREEN: Very light—"toothpick" quantity.

*LEAF GREEN: Darker than Mint Green. Pastels—"toothpick" quantity. Deep tones—¼ to ½ teaspoon.

*LEMON YELLOW: Pastels—"toothpick" quantity. Deep tones—¼ teaspoon.

GOLDEN EGG YELLOW: Much darker than Lemon Yellow. Deep tones only—⅛ to ½ teaspoon.

*ORANGE: Pastels—"toothpick" quantity. Deep tones—¼ to ½ teaspoon.

*BROWN: True chocolate color. Pastels—"toothpick" quantity. Deep tones—⅛ to ½ teaspoon.

*VIOLET: Pastels—"Toothpick" quantity. Deep tones—⅛ to ½ teaspoon.

ROYAL PURPLE: Dark purple; use ¼ to ½ teaspoon.

*BLACK: Use ⅛ teaspoon for grays and ½ teaspoon for deep tones of black.

Storing paste food colors

Paste food colors should last indefinitely without drying out, crystallizing or losing strength, if you follow these simple suggestions: Do not refrigerate them; do not add water, and store tightly covered.

It's not advisable to expose paste food color to bright sun or extremely strong artificial light over long periods. Certain climatic conditions may cause a semi-liquid to rise to the surface. This is more

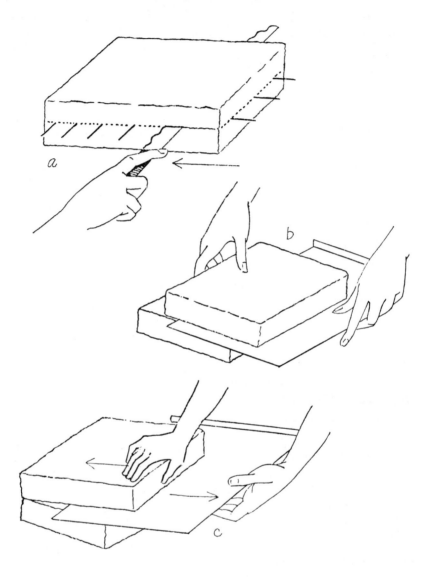

Fig. 8. How to split cake into even layers. a *Insert toothpicks at regular intervals; cut through cake above toothpicks.* b *To remove top, slip flat cookie sheet between layers with left hand, push top layer onto sheet with right.* c *To replace top after filling has been spread on lower layer, line up back edges. Keep top tilted as shown. Withdraw cookie sheet with left hand, pushing top layer into place with right.*

noticeable in Rose Pink. Stir before using. If the consistency is too heavy, thin with a few drops of glycerine.

Be sure the spatula or kitchen tool you use for stirring is clean and perfectly dry.

Buttercream Frosting No. 1

1 cup milk	1 cup granulated sugar
¼ cup unsifted, all-purpose flour	2 teaspoons vanilla extract
1 cup butter at room temperature	

Combine milk and flour in small saucepan over medium heat, stirring constantly, until mixture boils and thickens. Remove from heat and cool to room temperature. Cream butter and sugar until very fluffy. Add vanilla and cooled flour mixture. Continue to beat at medium speed until frosting is very fluffy and sugar is completely dissolved.

CAUTION: If buttercream is to be used for tube work, (borders, etc.), flour and milk mixture should be rubbed through a wire strainer before it is added to creamed butter and sugar. Yield: 3 cups; enough to frost, fill and border a 9″ cake.

NOTE: This is the best tasting buttercream I have ever used, a favorite of my family and students alike. I hope you will try it.

White Whipped Buttercream No. 2

2 cups white shortening	1 cup granulated sugar
1 cup sifted confectioners' sugar	1½ teaspoons vanilla extract
½ cup egg whites, unbeaten	Coloring if desired

Cream shortening and sifted confectioners' sugar in mixing bowl. Put egg whites and granulated sugar in top of double boiler over hot water; place on stove over medium heat and heat to 150° F. on candy thermometer. Keep over medium heat and beat to a stiff meringue. Press half the meringue through a wire strainer into mixing bowl containing creamed sugar and shortening. Beat on medium speed for seven to ten minutes or until completely blended. Strain remaining meringue into bowl, add vanilla, and beat about five minutes longer or until completely blended. Add coloring if desired. Yield: 4⅓ cups; will frost, fill and border a 12″ layer cake.

NOTE: You may substitute 1½ teaspoons meringue powder and 1¾ tablespoons water for each fresh egg white.

Chocolate Buttercream

1 cup sugar
⅓ cup water
¼ teaspoon cream of tartar
4 egg yolks
1½ cups sweet butter, soft

1 package (6 ounces) semi-sweet
    chocolate morsels
4 tablespoons strong coffee
½ teaspoon vanilla extract

Mix sugar, water and cream of tartar in saucepan and bring to a boil over medium heat. Cook to 234° F. on candy thermometer. In large bowl of electric mixer, beat egg yolks at medium speed until thick. Pour syrup over eggs in a thin stream while beating constantly. After all the syrup has been added continue to beat mixture until it becomes thick. Add butter in small pieces beating well. Combine chocolate morsels and coffee in saucepan and heat gently over low heat until chocolate is melted. Add coffee-chocolate mixture and vanilla to bowl. Beat thoroughly to blend. If the buttercream is too soft to hold its shape refrigerate it for about half an hour. Beat again to restore its fluffy consistency before spreading on cake. Yield: About 3 cups; will fill and frost a 9″ two-layer cake or frost and border a 10″ round cake.

Uncooked Buttercream Frosting

½ cup butter
⅛ cup light corn syrup
¼ teaspoon salt
1 teaspoon flavoring (vanilla,
    almond, lemon, etc.)

2 tablespoons milk
1 pound sifted confectioners' sugar

In a large mixing bowl, cream butter, corn syrup, salt and flavoring. Add sugar and milk alternately beating well after each addition. A bit more milk may be added if necessary to make a good spreading consistency. Yield: Will frost and fill a 9″ two-layer cake or frost a 9″x13″ sheet cake.

Decorator Frosting

1¼ cups Crisco
    or any white shortening
3¾ cups (1 pound) sifted
    confectioners' sugar

3 tablespoons water
1 teaspoon vanilla extract
Coloring if desired

With electric mixer at medium speed, cream together Crisco and 1 pound sifted confectioners' sugar. Add 3 tablespoons water and vanilla. Scrape bowl and beaters during mixing. Continue beating until completely blended. Add coloring if desired. Yield: 3¼ cups; enough for 25 roses or all the flowers, stems, leaves, etc., on several cakes.

NOTE: This frosting is used for decorations only. Thin (if necessary) by blending in a small amount of water, stiffen by adding sifted confectioners' sugar.

Always sift the confectioners' sugar when following this recipe. Scrape the bowl and beater often during mixing, but beat only until the ingredients are blended. Excessive beating after that only adds unnecessary air, so flowers and decorations are too porous. This not only detracts from their appearance but makes them fragile and hard to handle.

If you do a great deal of decorating you may find it convenient to double this recipe. It will keep indefinitely if stored in refrigerator in covered bowl or jar with a wet paper towel placed directly on the top of the frosting. Before using, bring to room temperature and beat again. One of my students kept some refrigerated for eight months; the only appreciable change she found in the frosting was a loss of vanilla flavor. By simply adding more flavoring and beating again she was able to use the frosting.

Creamy Frosting

½ cup margarine
6 tablespoons white shortening
1 cup granulated sugar
2 teaspoons vanilla extract
1 tablespoon cornstarch
½ cup warm milk

In large bowl of electric mixer combine margarine, shortening, sugar, vanilla, cornstarch and milk. Stir to moisten ingredients. Beat at medium speed about 10 minutes or until frosting is very fluffy and sugar is completely dissolved. (Rub a bit of frosting between fingers to be sure, as some sugars dissolve faster than others.)

NOTE: The frosting will appear curdled when it is first mixed. This is normal and will disappear as the frosting becomes fluffy. Yield: 3 cups; will fill and frost a 9″ two-layer cake or frost and border a 10″ round cake.

Boiled Icing (with Marshmallows)

1 cup sugar
2 egg whites
3 tablespoons water
¼ teaspoon cream of tartar

4 large marshmallows
3 tablespoons confectioners' sugar
1 teaspoon vanilla extract

Combine sugar, egg whites, water and cream of tartar in top of double boiler over hot water. Beat to a soft peak, then add marshmallows. Continue to beat until icing stands in stiff peaks when beater is lifted out. Remove from heat but keep pan over hot water. Add confectioners' sugar and vanilla. Beat to blend completely. Spread on cake while still warm. This icing swirls nicely. To smooth if cake is to be decorated, dip spatula in hot water when applying the icing. In humid weather, add 2 tablespoons more confectioners' sugar. Yield: Will fill and frost one 8" two-layer cake. If other filling is used, will frost one 10" cake.

NOTE: The addition of marshmallows to this icing will keep it from breaking down and "weeping" as so often happens with icings of this type.

Mock Marshmallow Frosting

2 egg whites at room temperature
¼ teaspoon salt
¼ cup sugar

¾ cup light or dark corn syrup
1¼ teaspoons vanilla

With electric mixer at medium speed, beat egg whites and salt together until foamy and white. Gradually add sugar, beating until shiny and smooth. Add corn syrup slowly and continue beating until frosting stands in stiff peaks. Quickly blend in vanilla. Yield: Will frost a 10" tube cake, or frost and fill one 9" two-layer cake.

NOTE: A sticky frosting which makes it ideal for use on cakes sprinkled with coconut and for lamb, bunny and snowman cakes where a fluffy surface is desirable.

About Royal Icing

Many of the decorations described in this book may be done using Royal Icing instead of Decorator Frosting. In most instances, however, I prefer Decorator Frosting because the decorations have a more natural look than those made from Royal Icing, which dries very hard and smooth. At times, however, this hard-drying characteristic is needed. It is ideal for figure piping and for trimming and finishing molded sugar works. It is also used as an adhesive where a non-edible substance would be undesirable. Decorations made from Royal Icing may be kept for long periods without deteriorating. The unused icing may be stored, covered and refrigerated, until needed. Just rebeat it to restore proper consistency. To prevent crusting over, keep covered with a wet cloth or wet paper towel at all times. Be sure all utensils used to mix and store Royal Icing are free from any traces of grease.

Although Royal Icing is sometimes used as an overall icing on Wedding Cakes, I prefer the taste of Buttercream.

Royal Icing Using Meringue Powder

5 teaspoons sifted meringue powder ¼ cup warm water
2¼ cups sifted confectioners' sugar

Combine all ingredients in mixer bowl. Beat at medium speed until a spatula drawn through mixture will leave a clean path. Yield: about 2 cups.

NOTE: See Sources of Supply for meringue powder.

Royal Icing Using Fresh Egg Whites

3 egg whites 1 pound sifted confectioners' sugar
¼ teaspoon cream of tartar

In top of double boiler over *warm water,* heat egg whites till they feel just warm (body temperature, about 96 degrees). Pour egg whites into mixing bowl. Add sugar which has been sifted with cream of tartar. Beat on medium speed of mixer until spatula drawn through it leaves a clean path. Yield: about 2¾ cups.

NOTE: Royal Icing made with egg whites will not beat up as well after the first time, so plan to use the whole batch once it is made. Drop Flowers made from it are good for cup cakes or other fast decorating jobs. After flowers or decorations have dried thoroughly, they should be stored until needed in covered boxes (see Sources of Supply) at room temperature.

Easy Fondant Icing

¾ cup water
7½ cups confectioners' sugar
3 tablespoons light corn syrup

¼ teaspoon vanilla extract
Coloring if desired

Blend all ingredients together in saucepan. Place over low heat stirring gently until mixture reaches 100° F. on candy thermometer. Add coloring if desired. If icing is too thick to pour easily, blend in a few drops of hot water. Yield: Enough to cover about 36 Petits Fours.

NOTE: If you have a great many pieces of cake to cover it is better to make up a second batch of icing *after* the first has been used, as this icing loses some of its shine each time it is reheated.

I am willing to go to lots of trouble for the sake of quality, but in my opinion the Easy Fondant Icing is virtually foolproof and is every bit as good as the conventional recipe which starts as a syrup, then is creamed with a paddle, and is once again melted down.

Petits Fours Icing Using Summer Coating

¼ pound (chocolate or pastel color)
   Summer Coating
7 cups confectioners' sugar

½ cup corn syrup
½ cup plus 2 teaspoons water
1½ teaspoons vanilla extract

Place shaved or chopped summer coating in top of double boiler over hot, *not boiling,* water. Let stand until melted and at 100° F. on candy thermometer. Remove from heat. With electric mixer at medium speed blend sugar, corn syrup, water and vanilla until smooth. Add melted summer coating and blend well. A small amount of hot water may be added if coating is too thick. Pour or spoon over pieces of cake as described in Petits Fours recipe (see Index). Yield: This recipe will cover about 42 pieces.

NOTE: Summer coating (see Sources of Supply) is similar to chocolate coating used for dipping candies. It is available in pastels as well as light and dark chocolate. (Do try the dark chocolate one; in fact, try them all!) All coatings except butterscotch have a mild chocolate flavor.

This icing is less sweet than Easy Fondant Icing in the preceding recipe, and has a candied quality.

Chocolate Fudge Frosting

½ cup butter
⅓ cup corn syrup (light or dark)
¼ teaspoon salt
½ teaspoon vanilla extract

1 cup cocoa
⅓ cup milk
3¾ cups (1 pound) sifted
confectioners' sugar

Cream butter. Add corn syrup, salt and vanilla; blend. Stir in cocoa. Add milk and confectioners' sugar alternately, beating until smooth and creamy after each addition. Add enough milk to make a good spreading consistency. Yield: 2⅓ cups; will frost, fill and border one 10″ round two-layer cake.

NOTE: When using for smaller cakes or in cake decorating, refrigerate extra icing in a covered container. Bring to room temperature before using. This keeps very well and is useful for quick decorating jobs as beating again is unnecessary. To use for inscriptions, thin slightly with a few drops of water, milk or coffee.

Fruit Glaze

½ cup sugar
1½ tablespoons cornstarch
¼ teaspoon salt
1 cup unsweetened fruit juice
or water

2 tablespoons currant, apple
or apricot jelly

Combine sugar, cornstarch and salt in saucepan and mix well. Gradually add fruit juice or water and blend. Cook over low heat stirring constantly until mixture boils and becomes clear. Add jelly and return to heat for half a minute, stirring until jelly dissolves. Spoon over fruit, filling tart shells to just below the edge. The Glaze will set at room temperature in about an hour. Yield: This recipe will cover fruit or berries in 12 large or 24 small French Tarts (see Index for recipe).

Orange Icing

⅓ cup butter or margarine
1 pound confectioners' sugar, sifted
1 egg

1 tablespoon grated orange rind
⅓ cup orange juice

Beat butter, 1½ cups of sugar, egg and orange rind together to blend. Add remaining sugar alternately with orange juice, beating until smooth. If too stiff to spread easily, add a bit more orange juice. Yield: Enough to fill and frost a 9″ square two-layer cake, or frost and border a 12″ round or 9″x13″ cake.

NOTE: For Lemon Icing, substitute lemon juice and rind for the orange juice and rind.

Fillings

Always be certain cake has cooled completely before filling. To keep creamy filling from soaking into cake, especially if filling is to be spread on split layers, first cover cake with a very thin coat of Buttercream Frosting.

Today as never before the homemaker has a wide range of convenience foods available. Cake fillings, or at least products suitable for use as cake fillings, are numerous. Puddings, prepared fruit pie fillings, cherry, blueberry, etc., make excellent quick fillings. Just open the can and spread on your cakes. Fruit preserves may be used by themselves or mixed with Buttercream Frosting No. 1.

Buttercream Filling Royale

1 cup Buttercream Frosting
  No. 1 or No. 2
¼ cup chopped pecans or walnuts
¼ cup semi-sweet chocolate bits
  or chopped chocolate

¼ cup finely cut maraschino cherries, drained on paper towel

Combine all ingredients in bowl. Blend well and spread between cake layers. Yield: Will fill a 10″ or 12″ layer cake. Half the recipe would be sufficient for an 8″ cake.

Pineapple Filling

3 tablespoons cornstarch
½ cup sugar

1 No. 2 can crushed pineapple, drained slightly
1 tablespoon butter

Mix cornstarch and sugar together in saucepan. Add pineapple, blend. Cook over medium heat, stirring constantly until syrup thickens and becomes transparent. Remove from heat. Stir in butter. Cool before spreading on cake. Yield: Will fill a 9″ or 10″ cake.

Strawberry Buttercream Filling

1 cup Buttercream Frosting No. 1   ½ cup strawberry preserves

Combine buttercream and strawberry preserves and blend well. Spread between cake layers. Yield: Will fill a 10" layer cake.

NOTE: Garnish cake with whole strawberries after frosting; whipped cream may be used instead of the buttercream.

Blackout Filling

¼ cup butter
4 tablespoons cornstarch
6 tablespoons granulated sugar

5 tablespoons cocoa
1½ cups confectioners' sugar, sifted
½ cup milk

Melt butter in 1 quart saucepan over low heat. Sift cornstarch, granulated sugar and cocoa together. Blend into melted butter in saucepan. Add milk and stir until completely blended. Cook over medium heat stirring constantly until mixture boils. Continue to stir and cook 1 minute longer. Remove from heat and cool. Add confectioners' sugar and blend thoroughly. Yield: Will fill a 9" square or a 10" round layer cake.

Lady Baltimore Filling

3 figs
½ cup walnuts or pecans

¼ cup raisins
¾ cup Boiled Icing

Chop figs, nuts and raisins into very small pieces. Blend into Boiled Icing. Yield: Will fill an 8" or 9" layer cake.

NOTE: Try this crunchy filling as texture contrast for white cake covered with glossy Boiled Icing.

Custard Cream Filling

⅔ cup sugar
3 tablespoons flour
3 tablespoons cornstarch
¼ teaspoon salt

2 eggs, beaten
2 cups milk
3 teaspoons vanilla extract

Mix sugar, flour, cornstarch and salt in medium saucepan. Add beaten eggs and milk. Beat with eggbeater until smooth. Cook over medium heat, stirring constantly until mixture boils and thickens. Remove from heat. Cover with plastic wrap to keep skin from forming. When cool add vanilla and beat in thoroughly. Yield: Will fill one recipe Cream Puffs or Eclairs. To fill 8" or 9" round layer cake, make up ½ recipe.

NOTE: For Chocolate Custard Cream Filling increase sugar to 1¼ cups. Grate 2 squares unsweetened chocolate. Stir into mixture when it begins to boil. Continue to cook till thickened and chocolate is completely melted.

For Coffee Filling add 2 tablespoons instant coffee to dry ingredients before adding milk and eggs. Omit vanilla.

Mocha Filling

1 cup strong coffee
1½ cups sugar

¾ cup (1½ sticks) sweet butter

Combine coffee and sugar in small saucepan, boil to 234° F. on candy thermometer. Remove from heat and cool. Place butter in mixing bowl and cream until fluffy. Continue beating and add cooled syrup a few tablespoons at a time. Beat until smooth, cool thoroughly before spreading on cake. Yield: Will fill a 10" round or 9"x13" layer cake.

Almond Cream Filling

5 tablespoons sugar
1½ tablespoons cornstarch
½ teaspoon salt
4 egg yolks, beaten

1 cup light cream
1 teaspoon vanilla extract
¾ cup almonds, blanched, chopped,
    and lightly toasted

Combine sugar, cornstarch and salt in top of double boiler. Stir in beaten egg yolks and cream, blending well. Cook over hot water, stirring constantly till mixture thickens. Remove from heat; add vanilla. If mixture is lumpy, beat smooth with a rotary beater. Stir occasionally or cover with plastic wrap to prevent a skin from forming while mixture cools. When cool, add almonds and spread between cake layers. Yield: Will fill a 12" round or 9"x13" layer cake.

Maple Walnut Cream Filling

Substitute 1½ teaspoons maple extract and ¾ cup chopped walnuts for the vanilla and almonds. Halved walnuts are a favorite topping for cakes filled with Maple Walnut Cream.

Grape Filling

½ cup grape juice
½ cup water
1 tablespoon lemon juice

2½ tablespoons sugar
1½ tablespoons cornstarch

Combine grape juice, water and lemon juice in small saucepan. Mix cornstarch and sugar together, then blend into ingredients in saucepan. Cook over low heat, stirring constantly till mixture boils and thickens slightly. Cool before spreading between cake layers. (Filling will become thicker as it cools). Yield: Will fill a 10″ two-layer cake.

Orange Date Filling

1 cup pitted dates (cut
  into eighths)
¾ cup orange juice
  (about 12 tablespoons)

1 tablespoon grated orange rind
2 teaspoons butter

Combine dates and orange juice in saucepan. Cook over medium heat, stirring constantly, about 10 minutes or until the mixture is very thick. Remove from heat and stir in orange rind and butter. Cool before spreading on cake. Yield: Will fill an 8″ round, 8″ square or 9″ round layer cake.

Apricot Filling

1 cup dried apricots, cut into pieces
2 cups water

½ cup sugar
2 tablespoons brandy

Cook apricots in water for about 30 minutes or until tender. Add sugar and brandy and cook gently for 7 to 10 minutes more. Cool before spreading between cake layers. Yield: Will fill a 9″ layer cake.

NOTE: For a Mixed Fruit Filling substitute 1 cup mixed dried fruit (prunes, apples, pears, peaches and raisins) for the apricots.

Lemon Filling

¾ cup sugar
2 tablespoons cornstarch
⅛ teaspoon salt
2 egg yolks, beaten

¾ cup orange juice and water
  (about 6 tablespoons of each)
3 tablespoons lemon juice
1 tablespoon grated lemon rind
1 tablespoon butter

In top of double boiler, mix sugar, cornstarch and salt. Stir in egg yolks, add juices and water. Cook over boiling water, stirring constantly until mixture is very thick. Remove from heat, stir in lemon rind and butter. Cool before spreading on cake. Yield: Will fill a 10" round layer cake or top 9"x13" sheet cake.

Orange Filling

1 medium orange
2 tablespoons sugar
1½ tablespoons cornstarch
¼ cup orange juice

1 tablespoon grated orange rind
2 teaspoons butter

Wash orange and grate the rind. Measure 1 tablespoon rind and set aside. Peel the orange and scrape away the white membrane. Break orange into sections and snip each section into eighths.

Combine sugar and cornstarch in small saucepan. Add orange juice and blend well. Cook over medium heat, stirring constantly until mixture boils and becomes thick. Stir in orange pieces and cook 1 minute longer. Remove from heat; stir in rind and butter. Cool thoroughly. Yield: Will fill an 8" or 9" round layer cake.

Blueberry Filling

2 cups (10-ounce package)
  unsweetened frozen blueberries
2 tablespoons cornstarch

½ cup sugar
1 tablespoon lemon juice
1 tablespoon butter

Thaw blueberries in a wire strainer over a bowl. Combine cornstarch and sugar in saucepan. Pour juice drained from berries into a measuring cup. Add the lemon juice and enough water to make ¾ cup. Mix with dry ingredients in saucepan and blend thoroughly. Cook over low heat, stirring constantly, about 10 minutes or until mixture boils and thickens. Stir in blueberries and cook 1 minute longer. Remove from heat and add butter. Cool completely before spreading on cake. Yield: Will fill 1 8" square or 10" round layer cake.

NOTE: To use fresh blueberries, sort over and wash berries then measure 2 cups. Place in a bowl and sprinkle with ½ cup of sugar or sweeten to taste. Cover and refrigerate for several hours or overnight. Drain fruit and measure juice. Proceed as directed for frozen berries.

Cherry Filling

1 cup (10-ounce package)
  frozen dark sweet cherries in syrup

1½ tablespoons cornstarch
2 teaspoons butter

Thaw cherries in a wire strainer over a bowl. Pour juice drained from berries into measuring cup and add enough water to make ½ cup. Combine juice and cornstarch in saucepan and blend well. Cook over low heat until mixture thickens and becomes clear. Add cherries and cook 1 minute longer. Remove from heat and add butter. Cool thoroughly before spreading on cake. Yield: Will fill an 8" or 9" layer cake.

NOTE: To use fresh cherries or strawberries, sort over and wash fruit. Remove stones from cherries and hulls from strawberries. Slice berries. Measure 1 cup fruit and place in a bowl. Sprinkle with about ¼ cup sugar or to taste. Cover and refrigerate several hours or overnight. Drain and measure syrup. Proceed as directed above. Or substitute a 10-ounce package of sliced strawberries for the cherries.

Chapter 4

DECORATING EQUIPMENT AND GENERAL ADVICE

Plan your decoration before you bake the cake, and be certain that both are suitable to the occasion. For a child's birthday, a cake decorated with clowns, toys, and animal characters is a long established tradition, like having vanilla or chocolate ice cream. Men and boys prefer cakes which features hobbies or sports, rather than flowers, but the bride will find enchantment in a cake decorated with blossoms that approximate those in her wedding bouquet. Consider season and sentiment too when you select the decorations. Daffodils are the essence of early spring; chrysanthemums of autumn; daisies spell innocence, and roses, romance.

Cake decorating is a craft and, like all crafts, you must practice it to achieve proficiency. Practice with a batch of Decorator Frosting (made up without the flavoring). Practice border and string work on an inverted cake pan; practice stems, leaves, sweet peas and drop flowers on a cookie sheet. Practice the other flowers on a square of wax paper fastened to the flower nail (see Sources of Supply) with a dab of frosting. Set the flowers aside as you make them to check progress.

To use the same frosting over again, just scrape it back into the bowl before it crusts over. Place a pad of wet paper towel on the frosting, and cover the bowl before storing in the refrigerator. Before using again, allow the frosting to come to room temperature. It may be used repeatedly.

84

Decorating Equipment
Bags, Paper Cones and Couplings

Decorating bags and paper cones have a similar purpose—they hold the frosting. There are times when one is preferable to the other, so try to have both on hand.

DECORATING BAGS are more practical for large amounts of frosting and making many flowers or borders, since they are easily refilled. Bags of plastic-impregnated or plastic-coated material are best. Plastic-impregnated bags (see Sources of Supply) cost about ⅓ more than the plastic-coated ones but give much longer service. Use the 10 inch bag for frosting, use the large bags (14 inch or 16 inch) with pastry tubes for pressing out cookies, cream puffs, etc. Canvas bags are not moisture-proof and are messy to use. Rubber bags are impermeable but are too stiff to handle easily.

PAPER CONES, which you can roll yourself from triangles of parchment, bond or wax paper may be used for all decorating work; however, they lose their shape after use and cannot be refilled easily. Parchment paper is best for cones, especially if they are to be used without metal tips, as for leaves. If you are decorating with several colors, make one cone for the use of each one. Paper cones are discarded after use and the need for washing is eliminated. For small amounts of frosting (less than ¾ of a cup) or for very fine writing, cut the triangles in half before rolling. This is economical and practical: the smaller cone is easier to handle.

To roll paper triangles into cones see illustrations.

COUPLINGS, which are sold separately, are used as adapters for decorating bags, enabling you to change the tips or tubes without removing the frosting. You simply unscrew the nut, change the tip, and replace the nut.

To prepare the bag for the coupling, cut straight across the tapered end, about 1″ down. Don't cut too much off—you can always cut more if necessary.

Pastry and rose tubes are used in the bag without couplings.

A metal cylinder with a plunger is *not* a good decorating tool. A decorating bag or paper cone responds much faster to pressure or the absence of it, making it easier to control the flow of frosting. You will learn as you progress that pressure control is perhaps the most important single factor in decorating.

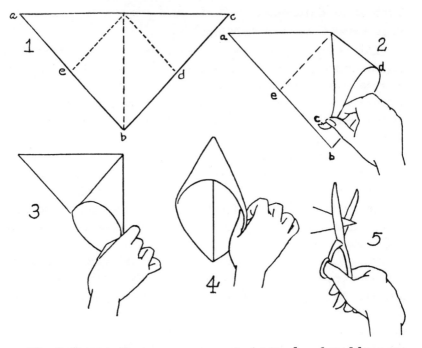

Fig. 9. Constructing paper cones out of triangles; dotted lines are roll lines. If a frosting tube is to be used, cut enough from tip of cone to expose ⅓ of tube (step 5).

Decorating Tubes

The number of recommended tubes (or tips as they are sometimes called), has been kept to a minimum, since the emphasis is on using a *few* tubes well. All of the designs in this book were produced using these tubes. Buy one each of the following (two each of 12 and 104):

Tube No. 2—For writing, and making very thin lines and tiny dots.

Tube No. 4—Same as No. 2 but for heavier lines, writing, etc.

Tube No. 6—For vertical lines in basket work and for any of the above uses where a still heavier line is needed.

Tube No. 12—The largest of the plain round tubes, for heavy lines and figure piping of large forms such as clowns, rag dolls, Santas and some animals. Since figures are made in assorted colors, buy an extra tube for a second bag.

Tube No. 16—Star tube for very small flowers, borders, striating sides of cakes.

Tube No. 30—Star tube for larger flowers, borders, etc.

Tube No. 48—Flat serrated tube for horizontal strokes in basket work and some drape work used on side of cakes.

Tube No. 79—For chrysanthemums.

Tube No. 101—For any of the above flowers in smaller sizes and for neck and torso ruffles on clowns.

Tube No. 104—Perhaps the most versatile tube; buy two, for sweet peas, pansies, daisies, small roses, buds, ruffles, etc.

Tube No. 126—Rose tube, also for large rose buds and daffodils.

Tube No. 131—Drop-flower tube for small six-petalled flowers.

Tube No. 140—Forget-me-not tube for tiny five-petalled flowers.

Round Tubes

No. 6—For drop cookies or plain round press cookies.

No. 9—For large plain cookies or cookies containing nuts or chocolate chips.

Star Tubes

No. 5A—For cookies, whipped cream, Old English Cheese flowers.

No. 6—For cookies, cream puffs, eclairs, and mashed potatoes.

No. 8—For large cookies, mashed potatoes, etc.

No. 9—Same as above, only results will be still larger.

No. 47 st—Used with serrated side up for bar cookies. Also with flat side up, for piping out icing in broad stripes of American flag decorations.

Other Useful Equipment

1 Flower nail No. 7—For all flowers in this book except lilies.

1 Lily nail No. 12—You will need one for each lily.

1 turntable or lazy susan—At least 12″ in diameter.

ICING SPATULA WITH FLEXIBLE BLADES

1 6″x¾″ blade—For icing small areas or cup cakes.

1 8″x1¼″ blade—For cakes up to 10″.

1 12″x1¾″ blade—For large cakes. This is optional.

6 watercolor brushes (from size 00 to size 5)—For applying glazes to cookies.

1 set paste colors (8 to 10 colors to the set)—Best for all coloring needs.

1 metal icing comb—For simulating pages on book cakes; it makes

close parallel lines across the top or around the sides of the cake when you draw it through the frosting.

Plain round cutter—About 3″ in diameter.

Heart cutters—In various sizes.

A pure bristle paintbrush—About 1½″ wide, for brushing loose crumbs from cakes.

A large knife with serrated edge—For leveling and splitting cakes.

CAKE BASES

Select trays, stands, and plates in shapes that approximate those of the cake but that are at least 2″ larger. Or make your own cake board as follows:

Select a corrugated cardboard circle at least 2″ larger than the cake. (For an 8″ round cake, use a 10″ corrugated circle.) Wrap the cardboard with aluminum foil, covering it completely; cut away extra foil from the bottom so the board is smooth and level.

For large or very heavy cakes, tape at least two thicknesses of cardboard together, with the corrugations running opposite each other (one running vertically, the other horizontally) for added strength. Tape together as many thicknesses as necessary to make a sturdy base, always alternating their direction.

For exceptionally heavy cakes, you may need masonite or plywood, cut larger than the cake and covered with foil.

Lacy doilies are not essential but they are pretty and festive under the cake. Select one that is larger than the cake but not larger than the base; buy the greaseproof kind if possible.

If the doily is not greaseproof, cut a piece of parchment or freezer paper about 1½″ larger than the cake; center the paper on the doily and fasten it in place with a few dabs of icing or piping gel. Fasten the doily to the foil-covered cardboard in the same way.

Hints for the Beginning Decorator

1. Before filling a decorating bag fold the top down about 4″, forming a cuff; this will keep the bag edges clean.

2. Fill decorating bag no more than half full. After filling, unfold the cuff and twist top tightly. Hold the bag in the right hand with the thumb placed around the twisted part. Exert pressure on the bag with the other four fingers. *Do not exert* pressure with the left hand. The left hand may be used as a guide but be sure to hold the bag down

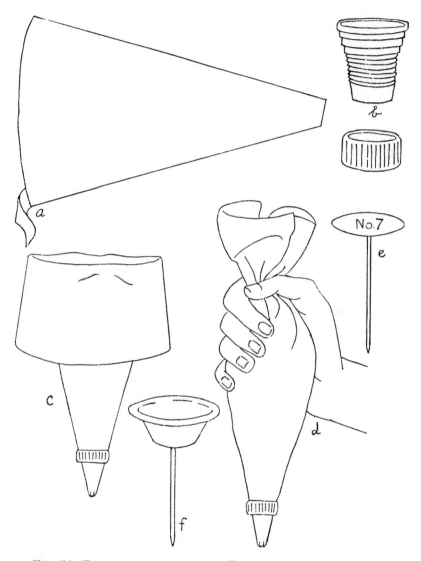

Fig. 10. *Decorating equipment.* a *bag;* b *coupling and nut* c *bag with cuff folded down;* d *filled bag with twisted top ready for piping;* e *flower nail;* f *lily nail.*

by the coupling so it exerts no pressure. Note: The left-handed person would of course hold the bag and exert pressure with the left hand using the right hand as a guide only.

3. After filling a bag, before starting to pipe squeeze some of the frosting back into the bowl. This will exhaust air bubbles and pack the frosting down tightly.

4. If frosting does not come through when pressure is exerted, or if it comes out of only part of the tube, it is blocked by a lump in the frosting. Clear it with a pin or a needle. If this fails, remove tube and wash clean with very hot water.

5. Decorator Frosting will keep indefinitely in the refrigerator. Keep some on hand for small decorating jobs . . . a real timesaver.

Assembling Cakes with Flowers

1. Place prepared cake (filled, stacked in layers, frosted, etc.) on a cardboard base. Pipe on inscription; add borders.

2. If cake is to have a basket, pipe it on next.

3. If stems are to be used in an arrangement, pipe them on next; add leaves if desired. On round cakes, shape the stems to follow the curve on the cake.

4. Place a bulb of green frosting, about ¼" high, wherever a flower is to be used. This enables you to raise the flower, rather than set it flat on the cake. Transfer the flower from wax paper to cover the bulb. Pipe on extra leaves where needed. If the arrangement seems to need more color or design, fill in with forget-me-nots or drop flowers.

5. For heavy flowers such as daffodils or chrysanthemums, you will need a sturdier support than the plain bulb of frosting. Snip a miniature marshmallow in half and place it at the end of the stem or wherever you want the flower to go. Cover the marshmallow-half with green frosting squeezed from a No. 4 tube; add flower at an attractive angle.

6. If you are not experienced in designing flower arrangements, study those you see in books and magazines. Use a minimum of flowers at first; you can decorate a cake effectively with just three flowers and a bud or two. A single long-stemmed rose in a vase made of piping gel would enhance any small cake. On the other hand, don't skimp on flowers when you are decorating baskets and large cakes. Remember, you make most of the flowers on wax paper first.

Fig. 11. Assembling a cascade-of-flowers cake.

Assembling a Cascade-of-Flowers Cake

1. Make flowers on wax paper squares two or three days in advance. The number required will vary according to the arrangement and the size of the cake. You will need about 12 to 15 roses, daffodils or chrysanthemums for a 10″ cake. The size of the flowers should vary slightly for a more pleasing effect.

2. Bake a cake at least 10″ in diameter. A tube pan is ideal. Frost with buttercream, reserving some for later use.

3. Cut about 24 rectangles, squares and triangles, each about 1″ or 1½″, from leftover cakes (the pieces left from filled Chiffon Cake, see Index, would be ideal).

4. Starting at center back, arrange pieces on top of frosted cake to form a crescent-shaped mound (see fig. 11a) about 2″ high at back and tapering to about ¾″ toward front (fig. 11b). Cement the pieces together with part of reserved Buttercream. Cover mound with remaining Buttercream.

5. Pipe several stems over mound and down the sides. Add small leave to some stem ends (see fig. 11c).

6. Place a large flower at center top of the mound (fig. 11c). Surround with other flowers tilted slightly. Leave space between some; nestle others closely together. Strive for an attractive back view too. Use smaller flowers at mound ends.

7. Complete cascade by piping leaves, drop flowers, buds or rosettes in some spaces between flowers. This design can perhaps stand a few more flowers than most but don't over-decorate.

Assembling Other Cakes

1. Place the cake (layers stacked, fillled, etc.) on a cardboard circle or cake base. Frost it smoothly. Add the inscription.

2. Add the decorations.

3. Pipe on the bottom border. If you are adding figures at the top rim of the cake (sitting clowns, for example), put the top border on *after* the figures, and only in the spaces between the figures. Otherwise, do the complete border.

Chapter 5

BORDERS, BASKETS AND LATTICEWORK

The cake border serves two purposes. It makes an attractive frame for decorations, and covers imperfections and gives uniformity to the edges. It would be difficult to estimate the number of border designs one could make. Three of the most popular and basic borders are shown in this chapter. When you have mastered these, the others will be easy.

Use any star tube for the following borders, depending on the size desired. The ones pictured were made with a No. 16 or No. 30 tube. For the average cake, the top and bottom borders are the same size. To make a cake look higher than it is use a larger border at the top than at the bottom.

Shell Border (Plate 1, row 1)

1. Attach a No. 16 tube to a bag of frosting. Hold the tube touching the cake at about a 60-degree angle (see Plate 1). Squeeze the bag, allowing icing to build up a bit in front of the tip.

2. Raise the tube slightly while maintaining steady pressure as you do so; return to cake surface.

3. Discontinue pressure altogether when you reach the cake surface and pull the tube away, ending the shell in a point. Start each successive shell at the point of the previous one and continue around the cake. Your first attempts may be a bit uneven, but practice will bring the uniformity so necessary to an attractive border.

CAUTION NOTE: Most beginners make the shell too thin all over, rather than heavier on one end as it should be. Correct by exerting more pres-

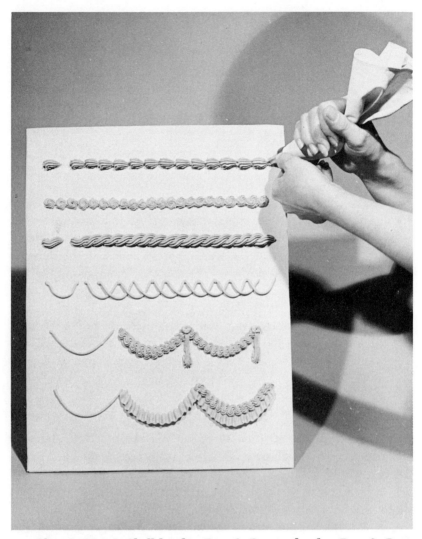

Plate 1. Row 1: Shell border. Row 2: Rosette border. Row 3: Rope border. Row 4: Single dropped string. Row 5: Garland with tassle. Row 6: Garland with ruffle.

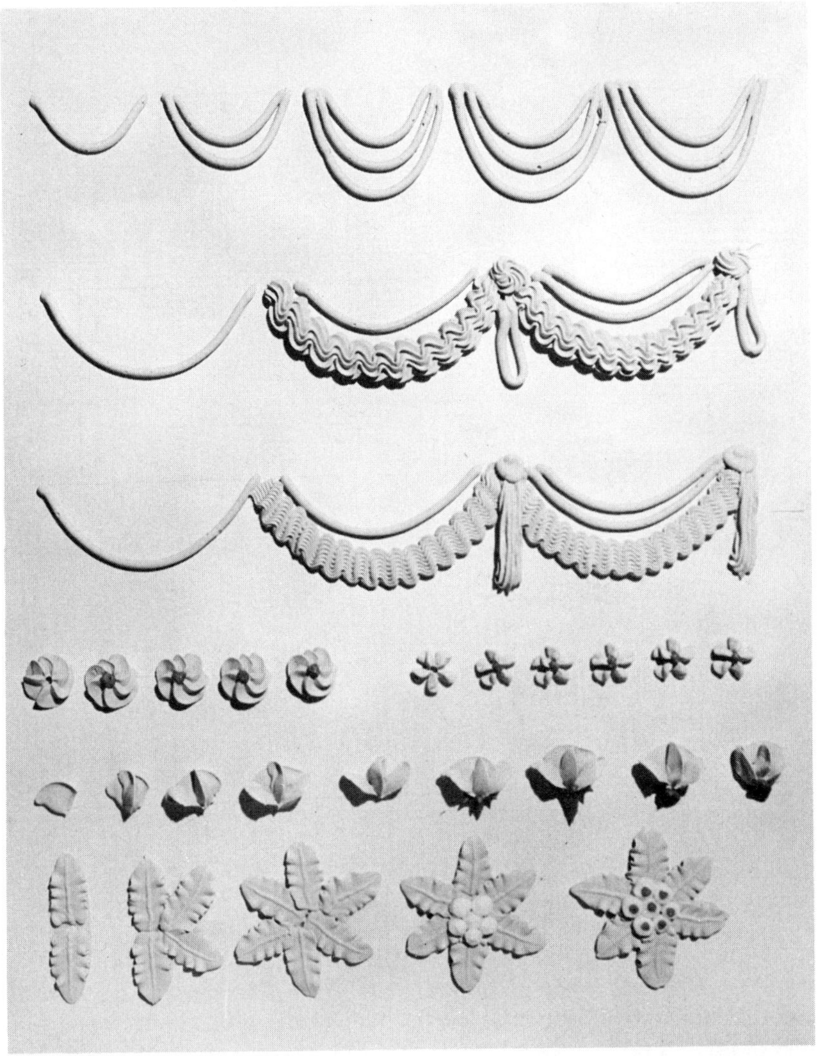

Plate 2. Row 1: Triple dropped string. Row 2: Garland, double dropped string. Row 3: Striated garland, double dropped string. Row 4: Drop flowers: forget-me-nots. Row 5: Sweet peas. Row 6: Poinsettias.

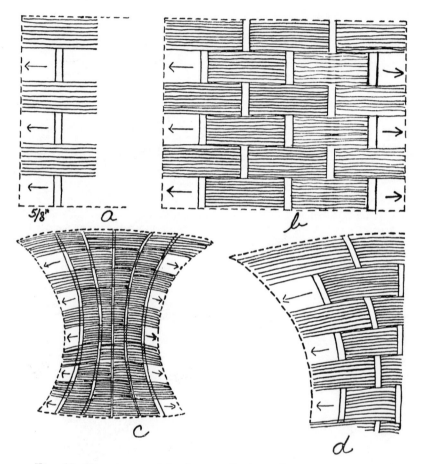

Fig. 12. *Two types of basket work. Straight sides* (a, b); *curved sides* (c, d). *Note that center vertical* (c) *is straight, others curve left and right.*

sure at the beginning of each shell. Also be certain to start each shell with the tube resting on the cake surface and at the proper angle. If the tube is held too low it will be impossible for the shell to build up properly.

Rosette Border (Plate 1, row 2)

1. Attach tube No. 16 or No. 30 to bag of frosting. Hold tube to cake at a right angle about ⅛″ above the surface. Exert pressure on the bag as you move in a small, counter-clockwise circle. When you reach the point at which you started, discontinue pressure but continue moving the tube around about another quarter turn. This will end the rosette smoothly rather than leaving a point of frosting at the spot where you cut off the pressure.

You can make attractive candle holders that match other decorations, using Decorator Frosting for single rosettes, pressed on wax paper. Press a matching birthday candle in the center of each rosette while the frosting is still soft. Allow them to dry thoroughly; remove carefully with a small spatula, and place on the cake.

CAUTION NOTE: If the rosettes have large holes in the center, you must either exert more pressure or make the circles smaller to correct this.

Rope Border (Plate 1, row 3)

1. Using a No. 30 tip held at the same angle as for a shell border, squeeze the frosting into what looks like an "s" about one inch long (Plate 1). Notice, though, that the curves are less sharp than those of an "s".

2. Start the second stroke touching the lower left half of the first one at the curve. Bring the upper half of the second stroke over the lower half of the first one, then come back to the left with the lower half of the curving stroke. Do not just interlock the strokes of frosting but actually cross one over the other as though you were twisting two strands of icing together to form a rope. Continue around, adding from the lower left half, crossing the frosting over to the right, and then return slightly to the left and toward you.

This border is a bit tricky, but well worth the effort as it is one of the most beautiful.

CAUTION NOTE: A common mistake is making the strokes too horizontal. Be sure to make shallow vertical S-curves on each stroke, see plate 1.

Basket Work

1. Etch the outline of a basket in the frosting on the cake top using a pin or other sharp instrument.

2. Fill two bags with frosting. Attach a No. 48 tube to one and a No. 6 tube to the other.

3. With tube No. 6, make a vertical line of frosting ⅝" inside the outline on the left edge of the basket. You will find it easier to keep the vertical lines straight if you squeeze out a bit of frosting with the tube on the surface of the cake to fasten it; then raise your hand slightly, lifting the string of frosting from the surface. Maintain a steady pressure and keep the string taut as you move to the bottom of the basket, touching the string to the surface when you reach the bottom. It is very important to exhaust all the air from the bag before starting the vertical strokes—hitting an air bubble would cause the string to break.

4. Holding tube No. 48 with the serrated side up, start at the etched line at the left edge of the basket and squeeze a ribbon of frosting over the vertical stroke and ⅝" beyond it. Leave the space of a horizontal stroke between them; continue making ribbons of frosting down to the bottom of the basket (fig. 12a).

5. Make another No. 6 vertical line, being sure it covers the right edges of the horizontal strokes of frosting.

6. Tuck the edge of the No. 48 between the first two ribbons of frosting and close to the vertical line. Squeeze out a ribbon of frosting and bring it over the second vertical line and ⅝" beyond it. Continue down to the bottom. Repeat this across the cake, alternating one vertical and as many horizontal lines as needed (fig. 12b).

7. Make last vertical line ⅝" inside etched line at right edge of basket. End horizontal strokes at this line.

8. Finish off left and right sides with half-strokes as shown by arrows (Fig. 12).

9. Finish all four sides with a shell or rope border. The border should serve as a means of straightening any irregularity of the basket. Strive for a straight border even though the basket may be a bit out of line. The border is what will catch the eye.

If a handle is desired, outline it first with a pin so it will be shaped attractively. Cover the line with the same border that was used around the basket.

Baskets that are to be completely filled with flowers may be left without a handle since the flowers would generally hide it from view.

To give baskets a three-dimensional look, fill in the outline with a star tube and the same frosting used on the cake top till the desired height is reached. The basket work is then done over this built-up form of icing.

Latticework

1. Draw freehand or trace the outline of the piece (heart, diamond, medallion, leaf shape, etc.) on a sheet of paper. Fill in the lattice lines. The lines should cross each other on the diagonal rather than at right angles.

2. Lay pattern on a wooden board or a heavy corrugated cardboard.

3. Place a sheet of wax paper over the pattern and stretch a piece of nylon net over the wax paper. Fasten all three together by pressing thumb tacks through all thicknesses and down into the board below.

4. Drop a No. 4 tip into a parchment cone and fill with Royal Icing. Carefully go over all lines in the design, first in one direction, then crossing in the other direction.

5. Carefully outline entire piece. The outline may be overpiped to give it more strength if you wish. Allow to dry thoroughly. When dried, carefully remove piece from the wax paper. Cut away excess net close to the outline with a small scissor. (A manicure scissors is ideal for this.) Turn piece over, face down, on wax paper and pipe over all lines and outline on the other side. The net will now be between the two sets of icing lines. Allow to dry thoroughly before using on cake.

Some lattice forms can be completed without the use of nylon net. Pipe the lines directly on the wax paper rather than on the net. This method is not so involved but the finished pieces will be a great deal more fragile. Net must be used, however, when all the lines do not connect, as in the case of butterflies.

Butterflies are made in the same manner except that each wing is piped separately without the body in the center (figure 13). When both sides of the wings have been piped and dried, carefully remove them from the wax paper. Bend a piece of cardboard, or better still a lightweight aluminum pie pan or T.V.-dinner pan, to a "V" angle

Fig. 13. *Latticework leaf and heart (top left). Butterfly patterns can be enlarged using graph paper. Where only one wing is shown, reverse for opposite wing.*

at which you would like the wings to stand. Put a dab or two of icing into the fold and press a piece of wax paper over it. With a No. 6 tube, pipe an elongated body into the bend of the pan, making it a bit longer than the center length of the wings. Insert the edges of the wings into the soft icing of the body. The sides of the pan will support the wings at the proper angle until the icing dries. After drying thoroughly, the wings will remain upright.

All latticework which has a three-dimensional quality so that it stands in relief, wholly or in part, must be made on net. Place the pieces in position on the cake after they have dried completely, and remove them before slicing the cake. These non-edible but decorative souvenirs can be stored indefinitely, and used again and again as cake ornaments for birthdays, anniversaries, etc.

Chapter 6

FLOWERS, STEMS AND LEAVES
(Wafer Paper Decorations Too)

Nearly any real flower can be duplicated in frosting. Here I have included those which are most often requested by my students. Some are simple; others a bit more complicated. Until you master the more difficult ones, decorate your cakes with drop flowers, sweet peas, or daisies. But practice faithfully, be patient, and before too long you will be producing the most complex floral patterns and designs. How gratified you will be when someone says "the flowers are beautiful and likelife. I've always wanted to learn how to decorate a cake!" Here is the method for drop flowers:

Drop flowers are easiest (Plate 2, row 4)

1. Attach tube No. 131 to a bag filled with Decorator Frosting.
2. Fasten a piece of wax paper to a cookie sheet with a dab of frosting in each corner.
3. Hold the bag straight up and down with the tip resting on the wax paper.
4. Hook your wrist in toward your body.
5. Begin squeezing as you turn the wrist out to its normal position, about one quarter of a turn.
6. Cut off pressure and lift tube straight up.

CAUTION NOTE: If petals cling to the tip as you lift it, do this: lift the wax paper from the cookie sheet. Attach a No. 4 tube to the bag and pipe parallel lines of frosting about one inch apart across the cookie

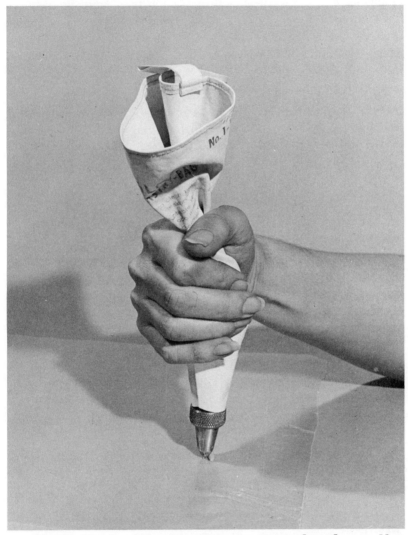

Plate 3. Hand and bag in position for piping drop flowers. Note how wrist is hooked inward toward the body.

sheet. Press the wax paper over these lines. Also examine the tip carefully. There should be enough space between the pin in the center of the tip and the teeth in it to get a pin or a knife tip between them. If there is not enough space, carefully pull each tooth away from the pin just a little. Replace the tip on the coupling and try again, centering each flower over the lines of frosting. If one or two petals still cling to the tip, some of the teeth will need to be pulled away from the pin a bit further.

COLORS: Drop flowers may be made in a variety of colors according to the flower you are trying to simulate. A violet would be made of purple frosting with a yellow center. Pale pink with a yellowish green center could be used for an apple blossom. White with a yellow center is used for an orange blossom. Two colors of frosting may also be placed in the bag at one time for two-toned flowers (see instructions for pansies elsewhere in this chapter).

Forget-me-nots (Plate 2, row 4)

This tiny but attractive drop flower is made with tube No. 140 and blue frosting. It is seldom used alone on a cake but may be grouped with larger flowers. It is also ideal for filling in spaces in a floral arrangement where the introduction of another color is desirable.

Forget-me-nots must be made directly on the cake.

1. Fill a bag with blue frosting and attach the No. 140 tip.

2. Hold the bag straight up and down with the tip resting on the cake.

3. Squeeze the bag gently until the petals are the desired size, then lift the tube.

4. Finish the flowers with a small dot of yellow frosting in the center.

CAUTION NOTE: Avoid excessive pressure on the bag to keep the petals dainty and separated.

Sweet peas

Make them directly on the cake or if you are a beginner, form them on wax paper up to three days ahead. In this way you can select only the best of them for use on your cakes. Always make more flowers than you need to allow for breakage when they are removed from the wax paper.

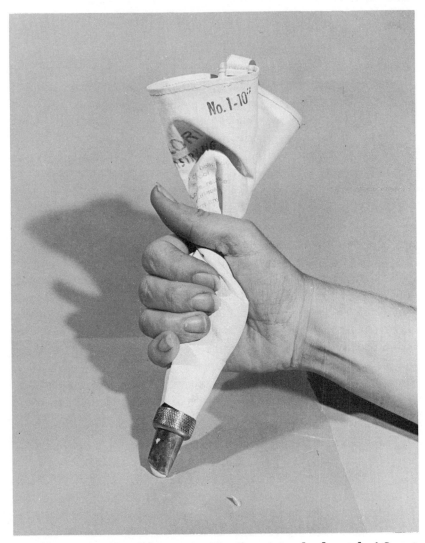

Plate 4. Hand and bag in position for piping back petal of Sweet Peas, also for Pansy petals.

1. Fill a bag with Decorator Frosting and attach a No. 104 tip. Rest the heavy end of the tube down on the surface and hook your wrist inward.

2. Squeeze the bag as you rotate the tip on its own axis. Give the thin end of the tip about a quarter of a turn to form a fan-shaped back petal. The thin end of the tip is slightly off the surface as it rotates. At the end of the fan, discontinue pressure completely and pull tube toward you. This will cut the icing off sharply.

3. Center the No. 104 tube on the fan-shaped petal, with the heavy end touching the base of the petal. The thin end of the tube should be a ¼" above the surface. Hold the tube in this position as you squeeze the bag and the petal will form itself.

4. Discontinue the pressure and lift the bag straight up.

5. With the thin end of the tube pointed to the left and a quarter of an inch above the surface, and the heavy end touching the icing at the base of the petal, squeeze to form another petal.

6. Repeat again, only this time have the thin end of the tube pointed to the right. After the petal is formed, discontinue pressure and lift tube straight up. This completes the petals of the sweet pea.

7. Finish the bottom of each sweet pea with a tiny bud vase and three sepals of green frosting put through a No. 4 tube, or a tiny green leaf. In either case, place the stem on the cake first, then add the flowers, and finish as was described. Use a water color brush dipped in hot water to smooth the end of the bud vase into the stem. Sweet peas are made in a wide range of colors including red, pink, white, purple, and yellow.

CAUTION NOTE: If the back petals are standing too high or appear too cupped, you are holding the thin end of the tip too high off the surface. It should be held just slightly above the surface. If the petals seem to lack the proper shape, you are holding the end of the tube too high from the surface. There should be only ¼" between the narrow end of the tip and the surface.

When sweet peas are made directly on the cake, the back petal may be eliminated completely.

Pansies (Plate 5, row 5)

Pansies bloom in a large variety of colors and combinations of colors, but for practice, one bag of a single color will do. Full in-

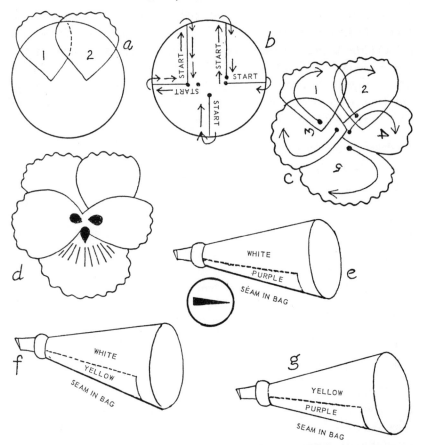

Fig. 14. Piping pansies. a *Spacing petals on nail.* b *Move tube in direction shown by arrows for each petal.* c *Note that the nail must be turned so the number faces you right side up as you pipe each petal.* d *Tear drop dots for faces.* e, f and g *How to fill bags for two-toned petals.*

structions for making two-toned petals and suggested color combinations will be found at the end of this lesson.

Cut some pieces of wax paper about 2½" square. You will need one for each pansy.

1. Fill a bag with Decorator Frosting and attach a No. 104 tube. Place a small dab of frosting in the center of a No. 7 nail and press a square of wax paper over it.

2. Hold the nail in the left hand, between the thumb and forefinger.

3. Rest the heavy end of the No. 104 tube on the nail and have the thin end slightly off the surface and pointed to the left. Start the first petal at the upper left portion of the nail (figure 14*a*). Squeeze the bag, moving it upward and slightly back and forth as you do so. Move upward about one inch, keeping the heavy end on an imaginary line (figure *b*). Turn the nail slightly and come back down, keeping the end of the tube on that same imaginary line.

CAUTION NOTE: There should be no space in the center of the petal, only a slight ridge in the frosting where the two halves of the petals meet.

Diminish pressure on the bag as you approach the bottom of the petal. At the bottom, discontinue pressure altogether and pull the tube toward you. Start the second petal to the right of the first one, taking care not to crowd it against the first one (figure 14*a*). Before starting the next petal, study all of the illustrations.

4. Turn the nail so petals 1 and 2 are nearest your right hand. Place the third petal so its upper half will cover the base of petal No. 1. Turn the nail again, this time so petals 1 and 2 are nearest your left hand and pipe a matching petal opposite petal No. 3.

5. Now turn the nail completely around so the empty space is at the top and all the petals are at the bottom.

6. Start at the left, pipe a large ruffled petal in this space, ending it at the edge of petal No. 3. The fifth petal, or the beard as it is sometimes called, is larger than the other four petals and will need to be a bit more ruffled.

7. The centers of the pansies are finished with teardrop-shaped dots of yellow or green Decorator Frosting.

8. For added variety some of the petals may be painted with fine lines of black paste color applied with a 00 art brush (figure 14*d*).

Pansies may be arranged on stems, in clusters, or in baskets. They are particularly pretty in baskets.

Allow pansies to dry thoroughly at room temperature before trying to remove them from the wax paper. Flowers made from dark icing require a longer drying time.

PANSY COLOR

To make pansies in a large variety of colors you will need about five bags with No. 104 tubes attached. Fill one bag with yellow and one with purple Decorator Frosting. The 3 remaining bags should be filled as follows:

Turn tube No. 104 on the coupling until the narrow end is in a straight line with the inside seam in the bag; you can check this by holding the empty bag up to the light. Using a small icing spatula or a narrow table knife, place a little of the color frosting you want at the outer edge of the petals down into the bag over the seam. Start the frosting strip just above the coupling and continue adding more frosting along the seam up to about 4" from the top of the bag. Make the strip thicker, not wider, as the bag becomes wider (Figures *e, f,* or *g.* Turn the bag over so that the seam and the strip of frosting are at the top. With a clean icing spatula, carefully fill the bag the rest of the way with the color frosting you want on the inside or bottom of the petals. Keep the spatula between the colors to avoid their mixing with each other. Another easier method of getting the second color into the bag is to squeeze frosting of the proper color into the space next to the color stripe from another bag. Fill the 2 remaining bags in the same manner, using your own choice of colors (or see color plates). For the largest variety of colors, make a few pansies from each bag, then make only two or three petals from one bag and finish the flower with frosting from another bag. For example, make petals 1 and 2 of a solid color, and the remaining petals two-toned. The possibilities are endless and you will be limited only by your own imagination.

Daisies and Black-Eyed Susans (Plate 5, row 3)

Daisies are white with yellow centers and black-eyed susans are yellow with a brown or chocolate center. They are both made in the same way; the only difference is in the color used.

1. Fill a bag with White Royal Icing or Decorator Frosting and attach a No. 104 tube.

2. Fasten a 2" square of wax paper to your flower nail. Use the edge of the nail as a guide so flowers are round and uniform in size. In the beginning you may experience difficulty spacing the petals if you try to pipe them in sequence. Piping them in the order indicated here will be easier.

3. Place the heavy end of the tube at the outer edge of the nail, and the thin end pointed at the center.

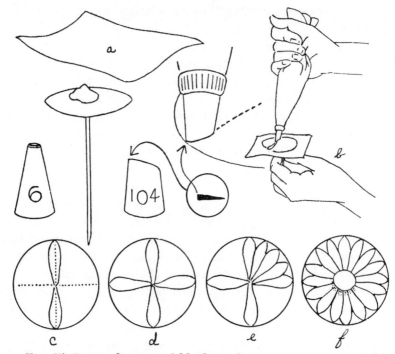

Fig. 15. Piping daisies and black-eyed susans. a No. 7 nail dabbed with frosting to hold wax paper squares. b Position of tube at beginning and end of piping. c, d, e, f Progressive stages in piping.

4. Raise the tube slightly above the surface of the nail.

5. Exert a gentle pressure on the bag. Diminish the pressure as the tip approaches the center.

6. At the center discontinue pressure altogether and pull the tube toward you.

7. Turn the nail completely around and pipe a second petal opposite the first one, dividing the nail in half (fig. 14c).

8. Turn the nail again and pipe a third petal between the first two.

9. Next, turn the nail again and place another petal opposite the third one (Figure d).

10. Complete the flower by piping three evenly-spaced petals in between each two already on the nail. The nail should have been divided into four equal parts by the first four petals (figure e).

CAUTION NOTE: If your petals appear thick and clumsy you may be holding the tube too far from the surface. The petals should be dainty and tapered at the center where they come together. If they are not, you are probably exerting too much pressure on the bag and not diminishing it enough as you approach the center of the nail. (This eliminates the excessive build-up of icing.)

11. Finish the center with a large dot of Decorator Frosting piped through a No. 6 tube (figure *f*). Use a yellow center on the daisy and a brown one on the black-eyed susan. Color a small amount of granulated sugar yellow or brown, as needed. This is done by adding a bit of paste color to the sugar and rubbing it between the fingertips until the sugar is uniformly colored. Moisten your finger and dip it into the sugar, then press the finger gently on the dot of icing in the center of the flower, thus depositing a bit of sugar which looks like pollen.

It is faster to put all the centers in the flowers at one time. Remove the flowers from the nail as you make them (keeping them on the squares of wax paper), and place them on a cookie sheet. Finish the centers and leave the flowers on the cookie sheet to dry. Any unused sugar can be stored in a small covered jar until needed again. Allow the daisies to dry thoroughly before attempting to remove them from the papers. In humid weather, allow more time for drying.

Always make more daisies than you expect to use; the petals are delicate and some will break.

Daffodils (Plate 5, row 4)

You will need two bags and tubes No. 126 and 101 to make daffodils. Drop a No. 126 tube into a bag without a coupling. Fill the bag with bright yellow Decorator Frosting.

Place some of the same yellow icing in a bowl and thin slightly by blending in a few drops of water. Attach the No. 101 to the coupling in a second bag. Squeeze a bit of the thinned frosting through it. It should come through the tip without your having to exert too much pressure on the bag, yet be stiff enough to hold its shape when ruffled. If it is the right consistency, fill the bag with the rest of the thinned frosting, otherwise adjust the consistency further before using it.

1. Fasten a 2½″ square of wax paper to the nail with a dab of icing.

2. Using tube No. 126, start the first petal at the center of the nail. Have the heavy end of the tip touching the nail at the center, and the thin end slightly off the surface, and pointed to the left. Press out a narrow, tapered petal by squeezing as you move the tube outward towards the edge of the nail, turning the nail slightly, and moving the tube back down to the center again. Discontinue pressure and pull the tube toward you.

3. Turn the nail around and make another tapered petal opposite the first one, dividing the nail in half (figure *a*).

4. Turn the nail and add two evenly spaced petals between the first two (figure *b*).

5. Turn the nail again and add two more matching petals opposite the last two. You should now have six petals fairly evenly-spaced on the nail.

6. Dip the thumb and forefinger into cornstarch and gently pinch the tip of each petal, pointing it slightly (figure *c*).

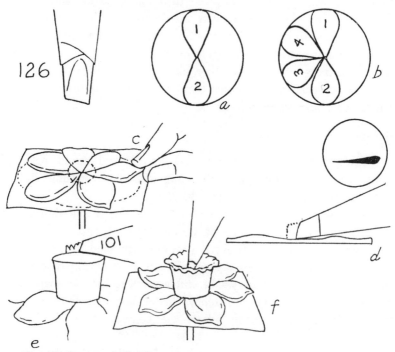

Fig. 16. Piping daffodils.

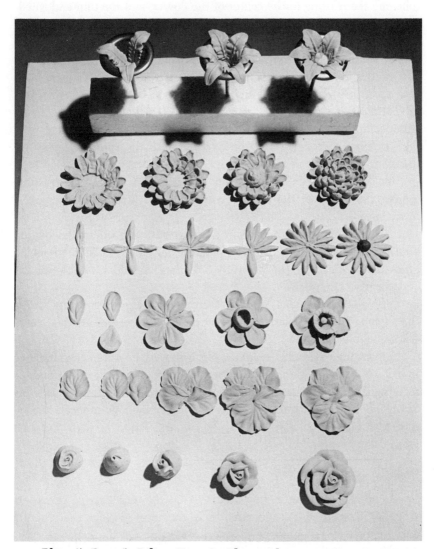

Plate 5. Row 1: Lilies. Row 2: Chrysanthemums. Row 3: Daisies and Black-Eyed Susans. Row 4: Daffodils. Row 5: Pansies. Row 6: Roses.

7. Hold the No. 126 in an upright position, with the heavy end touching the frosting in the center of the flower, and the thin end tilted just the slightest bit outward. Exert pressure while turning the nail counter-clockwise; form the trumpet in center of flower, fig. *d.*

8. Change now to the bag with the No. 101. Holding the heavy end of the No. 101 against the edge of the trumpet, and with the thin end horizontal, turn the nail slowly as you squeeze and work the tube slightly back and forth, ruffling edge of trumpet, (fig. *e*). If the trumpet appears to lean or be a bit misshapen after it is ruffled, dip the forefinger into cornstarch and gently push the ruffle one way or the other to improve its shape.

9. Finish the centers by placing small dots of orange frosting around the *inside* of the trumpet with a No. 4 tube or a cut parchment cone.

10. With the same tube and frosting add a pistil to the center of the circle of dots by exerting pressure and lifting the tube while gradually diminishing the pressure. The pistil should resemble an inverted carrot (figure *f*).

Allow the daffodils to dry thoroughly before removing from the papers. Brush away any remaining traces of cornstarch with a clean dry watercolor brush.

To arrange daffodils on the cake, snip a miniature marshmallow in half and place it wherever the flower is to be used. Cover the marshmallow-half with green frosting squeezed from a No. 4 tube. Set the flower on it at an attractive angle. The marshmallow supports heavy flowers like the daffodil whose weight would flatten a plain bulb of frosting.

Roses (Plate 5, row 6)

Learning to make a rose seems to be the ambition of everyone who has ever tried to decorate. It is the most widely used of all frosting flowers and perhaps the most beautiful. On the negative side, I must say it is the most difficult flower to make and perhaps the one that is the most often made badly. I mention this not to discourage you, but rather to make you more determined to learn it properly.

1. Drop tube No. 126 into the bag and fill with Decorator Frosting.

2. Fasten a 2″ square of wax paper to the No. 7 flower nail with a dab of frosting. Hold flower nail in the left hand.

3. Place the tip almost flat on the nail with the thin end pointing to the center. Squeeze the bag and begin turning the nail slowly, counter-clockwise. As the frosting begins to curl, slowly raise the tip into an almost upright position with the thin end pointed inward. Maintain pressure on the bag and continue turning the nail until you have an inverted cone of frosting slightly larger than ¾" in diameter at the base.

4. Place the tube at the top of this cone with the heavy end down and the thin end pointed into the center. Squeeze and turn the nail counter-clockwise for about one or one-and-a-half turns forming a smaller pointed cone at the top of the first cone. The entire cone now should measure from 1½" to 1¾" in height.

5. Holding the tube with its thin end at a point level or just slightly below the top of the center cone, and its heavy base tightly against it, squeeze gently, turning the nail slightly until a small petal is formed. Discontinue pressure but continue to turn the nail and the frosting will cut off. Repeat, making two more small petals around the top or bud part, the petals just touching. These first three petals form a triangle around the center of the cone. Start the next row of petals so that their top edges will be slightly below the top edges of the previous row, and flaring away from the center slightly, rather than being close to the bud as the first three were.

6. Exert pressure on the bag and turn the nail counter-clockwise. The petals are formed starting away from you and coming toward you. Go back and overlap each of these petals about a third of the way as you start them. Five overlapping petals are generally enough to complete the second row.

7. Start the third and final row with the heavy end of the tube resting on the nail at the base of the center cone. The thin end is pointing up and slightly outward. Squeeze the bag as you turn the nail, lifting the tube slightly and turning the tip out a little further from the flower as you do so. End the petal by bringing the heavy end of the tube back to the nail's surface. The bottom edge of the last row of petals may be described as almost half-moon shaped against the base. Overlap each of the petals in this last row as you did in the previous row. Five or six petals are all you will need.

CAUTION NOTE: If the edges on the petals appear ragged and

stretched, you are turning the nail too fast for the amount of pressure you are exerting on the bag. If on the other hand the petals are clumsy, ruffled or thick, the nail is not being turned fast enough. If the petals appear separated from the cone, you are not keeping the base of the tube pressed tightly enough to it. The thin end may be turned outward but the heavy end must be pressed tightly to the cone to fasten the petals properly. If the surface of the petals is porous instead of velvety smooth, the frosting is not packed down into the bag tightly enough to eliminate all the air bubbles.

I hope that you will practice the rose faithfully. Your reward will be the ability to make one of the loveliest of all flowers in frosting.

Chrysanthemums (Plate 5, row 2)

For instructions on how to fill bags for various color effects, see fig. 17.

1. Attach No. 79 tube to bag and fill with Decorator Frosting. Stick a 2″ square of wax paper to the flower nail with a dab of frosting. Holding the tube with the hollow part up, start piping petals about ⅜″ in from the edge of the nail. Squeeze firmly at the start to anchor the petals securely, then gradually diminish pressure as you move out to the edge of the nail, ending by pulling the tip up slightly. This will curve the end of the petal upward. Continue around the nail making slightly upturned petals which touch each other.

2. Begin the second row slightly inside the bottom edge of the first row of petals, making them a bit shorter than those in the previous row. These petals may be placed directly on top of the ones in the previous rows, or between them. The object is to keep the petals close together so the flower will be full.

3. When you have completed the second row, hold the tube straight up and down, and slightly above the nail. Squeeze a mound of frosting wide enough to fill the space in the center of the petals and about ½″ high.

4. Continue making rows of petals, starting each petal at the mound of frosting and curving it upward. The petals in each row should be shorter than those in the previous row.

5. When the space in the center is about the size of a dime, pipe five or six straight petals about ¼″ high in the center of the mound of frosting.

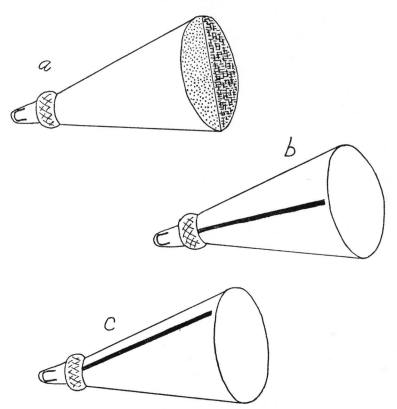

Fig. 17. Coloring chrysanthemum petals. a *For petals with a different color on each side, place frosting for underside in bag first (see hatched lines). Top side color is shown by dotted area. (Try bronze on top and yellow on the underside.) To reverse colors, reverse tip completely on coupling.* b *For petals with a contrasting stripe at center, paint brush stripe inside center front of bag as shown by heavy line. Fill bag with frosting.* c *For petals edged in a contrasting color, paint a brush stripe of color on one side of bag (inside, see heavy line) before filling with frosting. Note that the tube is held cupped side up each time.*

6. Pipe the last petals, wherever there is a space, pulling them toward the center and slightly over the short center petals. Allow to dry thoroughly before removing from papers.

CAUTION NOTE: If your petals, especially in the first rows, are flat instead of curving upward, exert a bit more pressure at the beginning of each petal; if the flower looks scrawny, you're not getting your petals close enough together.

Use a marshmallow base to support the flower on the cake.

Lilies (Plate 5, row 1)

Unlike the other flowers covered in this chapter, which are removed from the nail as soon as they are completed, the lily must remain in the nail or cup until it is thoroughly dried. For this reason, you will need one No. 12 nail for each lily you make. All lilies are made in the same manner; only the color is changed to achieve the different types. Some are dotted with a contrasting color after they have dried. The Regal, or Easter Lily as it is sometimes referred to, is pure white, with a center and stamens of yellow. This type is popular on religious and wedding cakes. I suggest that you try this one first.

The lilies must stand upright to dry so before you start use a nail to punch holes about 4" apart and in staggered rows into the top of an egg carton or cardboard box at least 2" deep.

1. Grease all cup sections of the nails generously with shortening before piping any petals into them. A No. 68 tip or a parchment bag cut as for a leaf may be used for the petals. If you are using a No. 68 tip, widen the opening to about twice its thickness. To do this, slip a knife blade lengthwise into the tip and rock it gently back and forth. This will allow more icing through the tip, making the petals thicker and not so fragile.

2. To pipe the lilies, fill a bag or parchment cone with white Royal Icing. Hold the nail in the left hand.

3. Starting at the center bottom of the cup, begin to press out a petal similar to a leaf. Extend the petal up the side of the cup, gradually diminishing pressure as you approach the top edge. Continue the petal slightly over the edge and pull the tube away gently, ending the petal in a point. Do not extend the petal over the outside of the edge of the cup any more than ⅛" as it may break off when the flower is removed from the nail.

4. Pipe two more similar petals, dividing the nail equally into three.

5. Pipe three more petals, only start these in the spaces between the first three rather than at the bottom of the cup. Strive to have the last three petals fill the spaces beween the first three, then begin to separate the petals as you round the top edge of the nail. When the flower is completed, stick the nail into one of the holes; let the lily dry.

CAUTION NOTE: If you have difficulty spacing the six petals evenly, mark the top edges of the nails with six evenly-spaced dabs of nail polish. Once dried, these marks will be quite permanent. You would then bring one petal up over each mark, skipping every other mark to pipe the first three petals.

It will take at least 24 hours for the lilies to dry completely. To remove them from the cups it will be necessary to heat them slightly by standing them in a warm place for a few minutes; the heat from the pilot light is ideal. Keep the flowers in a warm place until the shortening melts and becomes transparent. Hold the nail firmly in the left hand and give the petals a slight twist with the fingertips of the right hand. If the petals do not move, heat a little longer. It should not be necessary to exert too much pressure on the petals. When you feel that the flower is loose, turn the cup over on your hand and it will drop out. Treat the lilies as gently as you would fine china and you will have little breakage.

Finish the centers with a large dot of yellow Decorator Frosting and insert five yellow paper stamens (see Sources of Supply).

Poinsettias (Plate 2, row 6)

The poinsettia may be made with either Royal Icing or Decorator Frosting of white or bright red. As with the lily, a No. 68 tube or a parchment cone cut for a leaf may be used. Poinsettias are made on a 2½" square of wax paper fastened to a No. 7 flower nail.

1. Starting at the center of the nail squeeze out a petal that resembles a rather flat leaf.

2. Pipe a similar petal opposite the first one dividing the nail in half.

3. Pipe two petals to either side of the first two dividing the nail into six parts.

4. Using a No. 4 tube and yellow icing pipe a small, bell-like coil in the center of the petals. Pipe six more coils in a circle around the first one.

5. With a No. 2 tube and bright orange icing, add a dot to the center of each yellow coil, completing the flower.

CAUTION NOTE: Allow at least three days for the red flowers to dry because the large amount of coloring necessary to produce a bright red will retard the drying.

Stems and Leaves

Stems

Decorator Frosting for stems should be thinned slightly with water or a bit of egg white so it will flow smoothly from the tube. Tubes No. 4 and 6 are used for stems on flowers described in the preceding pages. Practice making them on a pan or cookie sheet before you make them right on the cake. Avoid using one large stem with many small branches. This is suitable for apple blossoms, but few other flowers.

To give stems grace curve them, bearing in mind that the weight of a flower on the end will cause them to bend a little. Study the illustrations for ideas on grouping.

Leaves (Plate 6)

I have found over the years that unless a very soft icing is used in making leaves with a metal tip, they will not terminate in a nice point. Leaves made from soft frosting are very flat and add little to a flower arrangement. This is the reason I prefer making leaves with a parchment cone cut to a leaf-tip shape. Leaves made in this manner always break off to a nice point and can still be pulled upward into natural-looking positions. Any size leaf can be made simply by cutting the tip of the parchment cone as large or as small as necessary. For just a few leaves a cone rolled from a half sheet of parchment is sufficient. Roll the parchment cone as usual but *do not*

Fig. 18. *Inscribe the cake before adding stems and flowers. It's easier to build a design around the inscription than vice versa.*

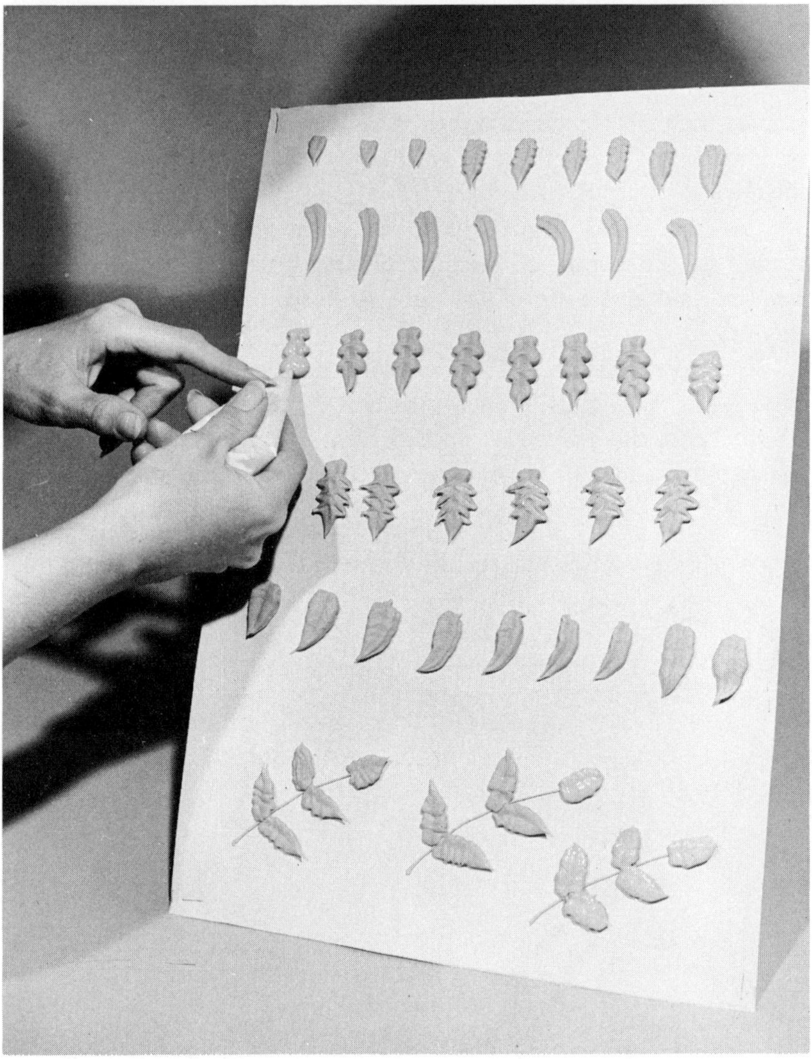

Plate 6. Row 1: Various size leaves. Row 2: Smooth leaves with only a center vein. Row 3: Jagged-edge leaves. Hand and cone in proper position for piping leaves. Note position of left index finger. Row 4: Holly leaves. Row 5: Larger smooth leaves. Row 6: Rose leaves piped on small stems.

cut the tip. Place a piece of cellophane tape over the seam at the back of the cone, extending it from the tip to about halfway up. Fill the cone with green Decorator Frosting and fold the top flap over. Turn the two corners down as shown in figure 19*a* of the illustration, then roll top down tightly. Squeeze the cone until the frosting is down into the very tip of it. Flatten the tip and cut to a "V" (figure *b*).

To pipe a leaf, hold the cone flat in the right hand with the tip resting on the surface of the cake or pan. The forefinger of the left hand is held at the tip of the cone to keep it flat when pressure is exerted.

1. Apply pressure to the cone with the thumb of the right hand, raising the tip slightly from the surface as the leaf builds up.

2. When the leaf is the desired size, gradually diminish pressure on the cone and pull it gently away, ending the leaf in a point.

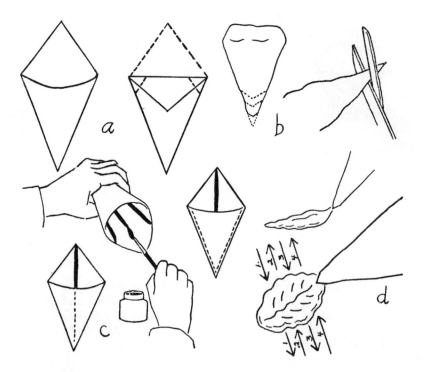

Fig. 19. Making leaves with parchment cone.

For leaves with horizontal vein markings, move the cone from side to side as you are squeezing. Complete the leaf by pulling the cone away gently.

Leaves with darker veins should be made my painting a line of paste color (green or brown) inside the parchment cone before it is filled with green frosting. Start the line at the tip of the cone and continue it up the center to the top (figure *c*). Holly and other leaves with jagged edges are made by exerting pressure rather heavily on the cone and then easing off in a jerky sort of motion that creates points on the edges of the leaf. When making holly leaves you can accent the points further by pulling them out with a fine art brush which was first dipped into hot water, fig. *d*.

Three-toned autumn leaves are made by painting the inside of a parchment cone with a stripe of brown paste color along one side, a stripe of green color in the center and a stripe of yellow down the opposite side, before filling with green frosting. The resulting leaf will be attractively variegated, *c*.

All leaves will be more attractive on cakes if you bring the tips upward from the surface rather than having them lying flat. Tuck the end of the parchment cone under the edge of flowers where possible so that the leaf will appear to be coming from beneath them.

Strive to add leaves to a floral arrangement in a natural way. Avoid placing leaves in a completely symmetrical pattern as this makes for a very unnatural effect. Where flowers are arranged in clusters, tuck leaves in between them. Do not hesitate to let a leaf partially cover a flower in a cluster.

Where a bright green leaf is not suitable, for example with daffodils, the green may be toned down by adding a bit of frosting the color of the flowers, a process called "graying."

Wafer Paper Decorations

Ready-to-use wafer paper designs are available for many occasions but do learn to make your own, for the times when you need a special design.

Cartoon characters so popular with children and young people can be reproduced even if you cannot draw a straight line. The design from paper party goods (tablecloths, napkins, etc.) can be duplicated on the cake using wafer paper. Coloring books are a good source of pictures because they cover a wide range of subjects and the outlines are heavy, making them easy to trace.

How to make wafer paper designs

Place a piece of wafer paper, smooth side up, over the picture to be traced; secure with paper clips to prevent slipping. Trace the picture using a Rapidograph pen (from art supply stores) which has been filled with a solution of water and paste color instead of ink. A tablespoon of water mixed with as much color as will cling to the tip of a toothpick is usually dark enough to produce clear lines. I prefer black for tracing, but any color may be used. A size 3 or 4 point is suitable for most wafer paper work. Remove the clips and place the

Fig. 20. Patterns for wafer designs; enlarge as necessary.

wafer on a cookie sheet. Paint the picture with icing or piping gel in appropriate colors. Next, outline the picture and go over facial features and accent lines with frosting or piping gel of the proper color, squeezed through a parchment cone with just a little tip cut off. Allow the picture to dry before placing it on the cake. The wafer sometimes curls or bubbles a bit as it dries but this will smooth out when it comes in contact with moisture from the frosting on the cake.

Wafer paper is edible so the picture may be cut with the cake at serving time.

Large forms traced on wafer paper may be cut out before they are painted. An example of this is the umbrella on the bridal shower cake. Cards with a message, such as the one used on the pansy-basket cake, are also cut from wafer paper. These are but a few of the uses for wafer paper; you will find many others.

Wafer designs painted entirely with piping gel may be made up months in advance without spoiling. Store them singly in a covered box until needed.

Chapter 7

FIGURE PIPING: FREEHAND & PATTERN METHODS

Freehand Figure Piping (Plate 7)

Clowns

Prepare the clown heads in advance as follows:

Mix enough yellow Decorator Frosting into about half a cup of pink Decorator Frosting to make a suitable flesh tone. Add sifted confectioners' sugar, a tablespoon at a time, until the flesh tone frosting is the consistency of modelling clay. Roll bits of the frosting into balls about ½" in diameter. Allow the balls to stand uncovered at room temperature for 24 hours, then store in a covered box or container until needed.

Clowns must be piped directly on the cake but may be practiced on an inverted cake pan that is at least 2½" inches deep. You will need tube No. 12 for the body parts, No. 101 for the neck and torso ruffles, and No. 4 for the ruffles around the wrists, ankles, and the hat. No. 4 is also used for the button, pom-poms on the hat and the shoes. These same tubes are always used but the order of use may vary according to the position the clown is piped in. The frosting used with tubes No. 101 and 4 should be thinned slightly. The frosting used with tube No. 12 should be stiffer.

If the clowns are to be dressed in different colors you will need a decorating bag or paper cone and No. 12 tube for each color but one color will do for practice.

POSITION NO. 1 (Plate 7, row 3)

Pipe clowns sitting at the edge of the cake with their legs dangling over the side.

1. Using tube No. 12 and Decorator Frosting, start piping the torso ¾" in from the edge of the cake. Rest the tube on the surface and exert heavy pressure on the bag while gradually raising the tube straight up. When the torso is about 1¾" tall and about 1" in diameter, discontinue pressure and pull the tube away (figure 21a).

2. Pipe left leg with No. 12 starting at the base of the torso, working to the edge of the cake and down over it for the knee. Continue the leg down the side of the cake about 1". Repeat for other leg (figure 21b).

3. Change to bag of softer frosting and tube No. 101. Pipe a ruffle at the lower part of the torso starting at the center back and slightly above the surface of the cake. Have the heavy end of the No. 101 against the torso and the thin end standing away. Make the ruffle by exerting pressure on the bag while working the tube back and forth, as in the ruffle applied to a daffodil trumpet. Continue the ruffle around the front to where the legs and the torso join and around to the starting point at the center back (figure 21c).

4. Place prepared head on top of torso. If it does not stick securely moisten the bottom with a bit of water and press onto torso.

5. To pipe arms, place tube No. 12 flat against the torso at a point below the head where the shoulders would be. With the tips of the fingers of the left hand support the clown on the opposite side of the body from where the arm is being piped. Exert pressure on the bag, fastening the frosting against the torso, then bring the arm away from the body about ¾" to where the elbow would be. Turn the tube back toward the body and pipe the arm about ¾" longer. Discontinue pressure and pull the tube away. Pipe other arm in the same manner (figure 21d).

6. Place tube No. 12 upright on top of the head. Squeeze the bag firmly so frosting covers the top of the head, then raise tube slightly while diminishing pressure. When hat is about ¾" tall, discontinue pressure and pull tube away ending hat in a point.

7. Pipe ruffle around the neck with No. 101 starting at the center back, continue around the front and back to the starting point.

8. Change to tube No. 4 and add a small ruffle to the bottom edge

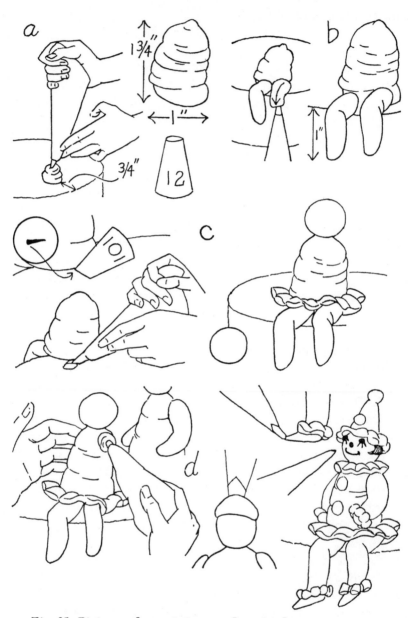

Fig. 21. Piping a clown sitting at edge of cake.

of the hat and a pom-pom on the tip of it. Still using No. 4 tube pipe ruffles at the ankles and wrists and add buttons to the tunic.

9. Pipe shoes using No. 4 tube. Starting at the heel exert pressure and move out toward the toe. Diminish pressure and pull the tube away, ending the shoe in a point. Hands are not piped on these small clowns because it would be impossible to get them tiny enough to be in proportion to the rest of the body.

Facial features are added using piping gel or frosting squeezed through a paper cone with a small tip cut off or a No. 4 tube.

POSITION NO. 2 (Plate 7, row 4)

Clowns piped lying on their back can be placed anywhere on the cake. The same tubes and body proportions as described previously are used.

1. The torso is piped first.

2. Start the legs at the base of the torso. Exert heavy pressure and lift the tube about ¾", then turn the tube downward to form the knee. Continue downward about ¾" to the surface of the cake. Repeat for other leg.

3. Press the prepared head into place.

4. Pipe arms and hat.

5. Finish clown as described previously.

POSITION NO. 3 (Plate 7, row 5)

Clowns in this position may be piped close to the edge of the cake with their arms dangling over the side and the head extended slightly over the edge or completely on top of the cake.

1. Pipe the legs first, starting at the thigh. Exert heavy pressure as you pipe the leg on the surface of the cake for about ¾", then turn the tube upright and bring the leg up from the surface almost 1".

CAUTION: If the leg doesn't stand upright you are not exerting sufficient pressure or the frosting is not stiff enough.

2. Pipe the body flat on the cake, starting at the thighs.

3. Press head into place as shown. Finish the clown as shown.

POSITION NO. 4

Clowns in this position are piped between the lower edge of the cake and the cake plate.

1. Pipe the left leg first, starting it at the cake plate close to the base of the cake. Exert pressure and bring the leg up the side of the cake about ¾", then bend the leg slightly at the knee. The entire leg should measure between 1½" to 1¾".

2. Pipe the right leg in the same manner only rest it entirely on the cake plate. Pipe the torso next in the right angle between the cake and the plate. The clown will appear to be lying half on his side and half on his back.

3. Add the torso ruffle next.

4. Pipe the left arm next, having it extended upward against the cake. The right arm rests on the cake plate. Finish the clown as described previously.

These are just a few of the many positions clowns may be piped in. Legs may be crossed and arms may be placed in various positions. Once you have mastered piping the different parts of the clowns you will be limited only by your imagination.

Rag dolls (Plate 7, row 1)

Follow the techniques used for clowns but note these changes. Use flesh-toned frosting for the arms and legs. Tube No. 104 is used for the skirt in the same manner as the ruffles are applied to the clown torso. Blonde curls are piped on using tube No. 4 and a hair bow is added using tube No. 101.

Santa Claus (Plate 7, row 2)

Follow the techniques used for clowns but note these changes. Paint the boots with black paste color after the legs have dried slightly. Tube No. 4 is used for the beard and the fur trim on the clothing. Tube No. 2 is used for the eyebrows and the mustache.

Pattern Figures

Trace patterns in fig. 22 using vellum or tracing paper. Lay on a cookie sheet or heavy cardboard and cover with a sheet of wax paper. Tack or secure in place with dabs of Royal Icing. Pipe figures on wax paper as follows. Allow to dry.

(Pressure control is very important in figure piping, so practice faithfully. The consistency of the frosting should be soft enough to flow from the tube smoothly, and stiff enough to retain shape without excessive spreading.)

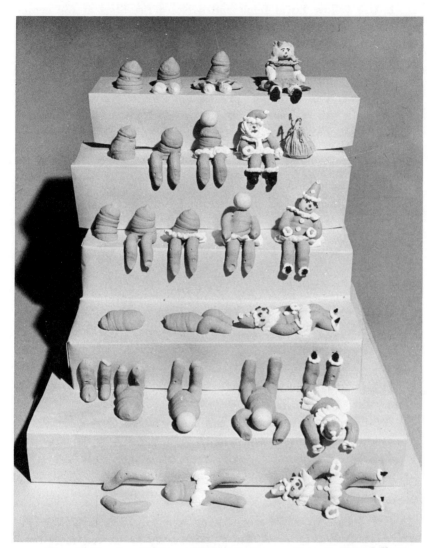

Plate 7, Freehand Figure Piping in Stages. Row 1: Rag doll. Row 2: Santa Claus. Row 3: Clown, Position No. 1. Row 4: Clown, Position No. 2. Row 5: Clown, Position No. 3. Row 6: Clown, Position No. 4

Large chicks

1. Use yellow Royal Icing and a No. 4 tip. Start at the center of the head and pipe a dot of icing large enough to fill pattern, keeping tip of tube below surface of the icing. *Do not* remove tube from dot of icing, but discontinue pressure on bag.

2. Gently move the tube (without exerting any pressure) out over the beak. This will move just enough icing to form a tiny beak. Remove tube.

3. Place tube at back of head, squeezing heavily as you move along the back toward the tail.

4. Discontinue pressure at base of tail but move tube along pulling a little icing to form the tail.

5. Move back toward head, exerting heavy pressure, and fill in outline solidly. The body should be piped thicker than the head.

6. To pipe wing, press tube below surface of icing at a point midway in body. Squeeze heavily just for an instant, then ease off on the pressure and pull the tube away, ending the wing in a point.

7. When the chicks are dry add a tiny dot of black icing for an eye and paint the beaks with orange color.

NOTE: To avoid breakage *do not* pipe legs and feet until after the chicks are placed on an egg or cake.

Clown

1. Use Royal Icing in appropriate colors and tube No. 4. Pipe a round dot for the head.

2. Fill in the torso and add the hands, feet, and ruffles next.

3. Start hat at the crown and taper to a point at the tip.

4. Add buttons and facial features after the figure has dried completely to avoid bleeding of colors.

Ducks

Use yellow or white Royal Icing and tube No. 4. Follow the same procedure as for chicks but pipe the body by exerting more pressure for a heavier build-up of icing. As with chicks, the legs are added after the duck is placed on an egg or cake.

Boy, girl, and clown head

1. Use tube No. 4 and Royal Icing in appropriate colors. Pipe a large round dot in flesh tone or pink.

Fig. 22. Pattern figures to trace.

2. Allow to dry before adding hair, eyes, nose, ruffles, etc.

Mouse and tiger heads

1. Use tube No. 4 and Royal Icing in appropriate colors. Pipe ears first, starting at the top and working down.

2. Pipe the heads on next, exerting enough pressure on the cone to cause the icing to spread and fill the outline of the pattern. The tip of the tube should be below the surface when piping the heads.

3. Add features and accent markings after the icing has dried completely.

Large duckling and chick

1. Use a No. 6 tube for larger areas and a No. 4 tube for smaller areas. Fill all areas of one color at a time, then start using another color. Keep tip of tube below the surface of the icing, especially when filling in the larger areas.

2. Add eyes and accents after drying. Legs and feet are put on after the piece has been placed on the cake. If the figures are not to be used immediately, store them without removing from the paper to avoid breakage.

Tiny chicks

Use yellow Royal Icing and No. 2 tube. Proceed as for larger chicks.

Any of these Royal Icing figures may be stored for future use. For best results do not remove from paper until needed. Store covered and in a dry place.

Rabbits

1. Use brown or white Royal Icing and a No. 4 tip. Pipe the ears first, starting at the top.

2. Start piping the head at the nose and moving upward, covering the ends of the ears.

3. Fill in the body, starting below the head and moving outward to the end of the foreleg.

4. Pipe the hind leg, exerting more pressure on the cone to give a three-dimensional look to the haunches.

5. Pipe the tail last. Features are piped on when the rabbit is dried. A small orange carrot with a green top may be added at the tip of the foreleg at this time if desired.

Chapter 8

STRINGS, GARLANDS AND INSCRIPTIONS

Strings (Plates 1 and 2)

String work is used primarily on the sides of wedding cake tiers, but do try it on cakes for other festive occasions. Royal Icing is considered best for string work but I have had equal success using Buttercream. In fact, most of the string work on the wedding cakes shown in color was done using Buttercream.

Drop a No. 4 tube into a parchment bag or attach to coupling on a decorating bag. Fill the bag with Royal Icing or Buttercream. Squeeze some of the icing out of the bag to exhaust any air bubbles and pack the icing tightly. This is important because even a small pocket of air in the bag could cause the string to break.

A cake pan at least three inches deep may be used to practice on before you attempt to do any string work on a cake. Elevate the pan to eye level by placing it on a turntable or lazy susan set, if necessary, on a pot or cardboard box.

Start the first string slightly to your left rather than directly in front of you. Hold the tube against the pan and squeeze a little to anchor the icing to it. Maintain a steady pressure on the cone while moving the hand along the top edge of the pan about 1½", allowing the string of icing to drop down about 1" below the top edge of the pan. Fasten the icing by touching the tip to the top edge of the pan and discontinuing pressure on the cone. See plate 1, row 4 Chapter 5.

Triple Dropped string (Plate 2, row 1, chapter 8)

Use tube No. 4 or 6. This design is almost self-explanatory. A series of three strings is dropped one below the other, then the next three are started next to them.

CAUTION NOTE: Most beginners drop the hand as the icing string drops but this makes it impossible to get smooth, uniform drops. Keep the hand moving along the top edge of the pan and let gravity pull the icing string down. When it has dropped the proper distance, touch the tip to the top edge of the pan to fasten it and start the next drop or loop. Before going on to more intricate designs, practice getting a series of single drops completely uniform. String work is not difficult but it requires a certain amount of rhythm which only practice can provide. This is the basis of all string work, so after you have mastered it the rest will come easily.

Garlands

Garland work is done using string-work loops spaced 2" to 2½" apart as a guide. If you are not able to do string work with this much space between the loops, try marking your cake this way: use a doughnut cutter with the center removed, or a biscuit or cookie cutter about 3" in diameter. Mark both sides of the cutter by dabbing nail polish or scratching the halfway point. Have these marks at the top edge of the cake as you press the cutter into the frosting on the cake, marking half circles in it. Continue about ⅔ of the way around the tier. At this point check to see how many more half circles you will have room for. (Or test on a cardboard circle which is the same size as your cake.) It may be necessary to space them a little further apart or squeeze them a little closer together. The object is to avoid ending up with a space too large for one garland but not large enough for two, and by looking ahead, you can eliminate this possibility. A slight variation in the size of the garlands won't be noticeable in the finished cake.

Garland with tassle (Plate 1, row 5, chapter 8)

1. Mark garlands as described above. Cover marks with up and down motion of No. 16 or No. 30.

2. Make tassels in between garlands by piping an elongated inverted shell (about 2" long) with a No. 16 or No. 30.

Garland with ruffle (Plate 1, row 6, chapter 8)

1. Pipe the ruffle with tube No. 104 in and up and down motion, touching the guideline with thick end and holding thin end down and away from cake.

2. Pipe a No. 30 garland over top edge of ruffle.

3. A small circle may be piped where each two garlands come together using No. 6 or No. 16. The circles are added *after* the top border is applied to the cake.

Garland with double dropped string (Plate 2, row 2)

1. Mark and pipe the garlands as described previously, using No. 16 or 30.

2. Pipe the double strings and the string loops between garlands with No. 4 or No. 6.

3. Add circles on top of loops with No. 6 or 16 *after* the top border has been piped on the cake.

Striated garland with double dropped string (Plate 2, row 3)

1. Mark garlands. Pipe over marks with a No. 48 serrated side up. Move tube in a motion similar to making a ruffle.

2. Drop the double string above the garland with tube No. 6.

3. Pipe tassles as decribed above, using No. 16 or 30, pipe circles above tassels using No. 6 or 16.

Inscriptions

I find it easier to do very fine writing using just a small parchment cone with a tiny bit of the tip cut off, but if you prefer a metal tip, use tubes No. 2 or 4 in parchment cones. Place the tip in a small parchment cone rather than in a decorating bag. Since you do not use coupling, you can get your hand closer to the cake's surface, making it easier to control the flow of frosting or piping gel.

If frosting is used, it should be thinned down with water or egg white so it will be soft enough to flow through a very fine opening without too much pressure on the cone. Piping gel is suitable for writing, because it is the right consistency and seldom lumps. The shiny glasslike finish is attractive on a cake.

The writing style is largely a matter of taste, but here again, good judgment should prevail. You would not think of using Old English lettering on a cake with clowns any more than you would use the up-and-down type of lettering so popular for children's cakes for a quotation from the Bible.

As to technique, the same rules apply to all writing styles. The

Fig. 23. Lettering and inscriptions.

substance should flow smoothly from the tips. The tip must lightly skim the surface of the cake while you are writing. This is essential because it is impossible to control the flow if the tip is off the surface. It will require a bit of practice before you are able to skim over the surface and yet not gouge the surface with the tip.

Spacing is also very important. In the beginning, do not use inscriptions which are centered on the cake. Off-center inscriptions are easier for the beginner but care is still necessary. Be sure to start the inscription far enough to the left of the cake so it will not be necessary to crowd the letters as you approach the right. Bear in mind that, on round cakes, the center is the widest point, so plan to put long words such as "Congratulations" or "Anniversary" on this part of the cake.

Where inscriptions must be centered, count the letters. Allow for a space between each letter and a larger space between words. It is a good practice to write out your inscription on paper, using the proper spacing, then copy it. Even the best spellers have been horrified at one time or another upon realizing too late that they had left a letter out of a word on a cake.

Avoid straight square block letters because the slightest imperfections show up in this type of inscription.

By adding a little interest to your letters, you can draw attention away from any flaws which might otherwise stand out (figure 23). Notice how the second stroke of the "h" is pulled down a bit lower than the first. Bringing the down-stroke of the "R" down lower and under the following letter is helpful.

I do not recommend etching inscriptions on the cake with a pin or toothpick because the gouge in the icing will almost always show. Instead, if you feel you must pre-write, try this: Use a parchment cone of frosting or gel with just the tiniest tip cut off. The opening should allow through it frosting only about the thickness of a sharpened pencil-lead. Write the inscription with this. The thread may break here and there because it is so thin, but it will give you a guideline of sorts. Cut the opening larger and go over the inscription, making whatever improvements seem necessary as you do so.

If you ever have need to put an inscription on the sides of a cake, be sure to elevate the cake so you will be writing at eye level; otherwise, it is very difficult to keep the lettering straight.

Study the color illustrations of the different styles of writing and lettering and choose the one that best suits the cake you are planning.

CAUTION NOTE: Practice lettering or try out the actual inscription on a sheet of wax paper cut to the size of the cake. To reuse frosting, scrape back into bowl before it crusts. Note how letters may be piped one above the other to save space. Figure 23 shows a simple alphabet and art nouveau styles for teenagers. Figure 24 shows the dimensions of an easily-constructed hand support.

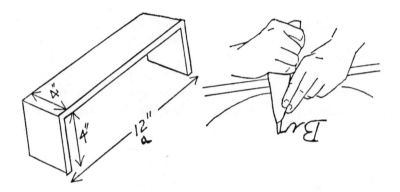

Fig. 24. An easy-to-build writing aid for those whose hands are not steady. Construct it of plywood or 1" x 4" boards.

Chapter 9

MAKING WEDDING, TIER AND DOLL CAKES

Most types of cake batter can be used in tier cakes. My own favorite is a rich butter cake.

For your first wedding cake, it might be best to use round tiers rather than square ones, as they are easier to frost. Choose pan sizes having a 3″ or 4″ difference between them. A 3″ difference is best when the flowers are spiralled up the sides of the tiers. Tiers with only a 2″ difference do not have enough setback to be attractive. The cakes should be baked at least two days in advance, as a too-fresh cake is difficult to cut and will also tend to settle a bit, giving the cake a lop-sided appearance.

The decorations on wedding cakes include a great many varied techniques. If you have practiced and mastered the ones described earlier, you should be able to decorate a wedding cake of your own design, or duplicate one of those pictured in color.

Select a board or tray at least 6″ larger than the bottom tier of the cake. This can be trimmed with pleated ribbon and net or covered with doilies. Greaseproof doilies are best, but if you must use regular paper doilies, do the following: glue them to the board or tray with dabs of piping gel. Cut a circle of parchment or freezer paper about 1½″ larger than the bottom tier and fasten it, centered on the board. This extra ¾″ will accommodate the border and no icing will come in contact with the doilies.

Before filling the tiers, compare them as to height. The bottom

141

tier should be the highest. Each succeeding tier should be a bit lower. To have all the tiers the same height would cause the upper ones to look higher than the lower ones and spoil the visual balance of the cake. The smaller the tier, the higher it will appear.) Don't hesitate to trim off a bit of the cake if the cake seems unbalanced.

Spread a fruit filling or Buttercream between the layers of each tier. Put a dab of frosting on a corrugated circle and place the cake tier on this. Repeat with each tier. If the cardboard circle is slightly larger than the cake, cut away the excess with a large scissors.

Cover each tier with a thin coat of Buttercream and allow to stand overnight, or at least several hours before applying the finish coat of frosting.

Wedding cakes can be decorated completely in white, but color is acceptable and attractive. The colors used should be kept light, so mix them carefully. Bright red is often chosen for Christmas or Valentine's Day weddings but the choice of color, or its absence, should be left to the bride.

Plan your cake with a definite theme, so that the decorations on each tier will all be related. If you use roses and bells on one tier, don't use hearts and slippers on another. The four motifs are appropriate on wedding cakes, but never all on the same cake.

Place flowers on the cake with a design in mind, perhaps in groups of two or three equally distant around the tiers, or spiralled up the sides. Never place the flowers here and there at random. They will be easier to arrange if allowed to dry thoroughly before they are used. If fresh flowers are to be used on the cake, do not use icing flowers also.

String and garland work, if used, should be proportioned for each tier. Use dainty designs on the upper tiers and gradually heavier ones on the lower tiers. These designs are preferably done in the same color as the overall frosting, but may be done in some other color.

The White Whipped Buttercream may be made in advance but omit the flavoring. Before use, rebeat it to make it fluffy and add the flavoring.

Assembling the Cake

To keep the lower tiers from being crushed by the weight of the upper tiers, it is necessary to support them. Buy a few lengths of ¼″ wooden dowels from a lumberyard. Wipe them clean and let dry thoroughly before using them.

Place the bottom tier on the turntable and frost it smoothly, especially at the sides. (Most of the top will be covered by the next tier.) Spread some icing or piping gel in the center of the prepared board or tray and carefully transfer the frosted tier to it.

Push a piece of dowel down into the center of the tier until it hits the board beneath it. Carefully pull out the dowel, then cut it off at the spot where some icing clings to it, using a pair of garden pruning shears or a sharp kitchen knife. Cut four other pieces the same length. Replace one piece in the hole at the center of the tier and space the other four 2″ from the edge of an imaginary circle the size of the next tier. (See figs. 25*a*, 25*b*).

Frost the remaining tiers one at a time. Dowel them, measuring the length of the dowel for each tier (this will vary from tier to tier), and center them on the tier below. It usually is not necessary to dowel the two topmost tiers as they are seldom heavy enough to crush each other. However, if the top tier is fruit cake it will be necessary to dowel the tier below it.

After the cake is completely frosted and assembled, begin to decorate it. If you are using string or garland work on the sides of the tiers, add it next, before the borders. If the cake is being completed without side decorations, the borders may be put on first. I prefer to start working on the top tier and work down, away from the completed tiers.

Add the flowers and leaves after all the borders are completed. It may be necessary to squeeze a bulb of white frosting where you intend to place the flowers, so as to hold them. If this is done carefully, it won't be visible after the flowers are in place. Leaves may be made from icing or silver foil, or green wafer leaves may be used. If the flowers on the cake are white, I recommend the use of silver leaves; green would present too much of a contrast, and white leaves wouldn't show the flowers off to any advantage. Daisies, however, are attractive with green leaves.

A final word of advice on decorating wedding cakes at home. Allow plenty of time. Do as many things as possible in advance. Be sure to make more flowers than you plan to use, to provide for break-

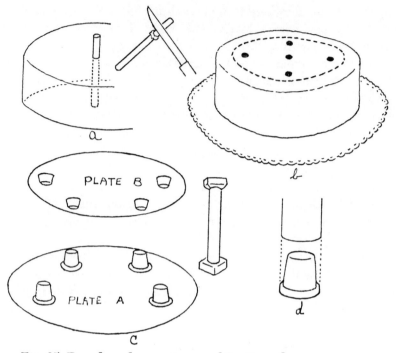

Fig. 25. *Dowels and separators used for tier cakes.*

Fig. 26. Cutting tier and other cakes. a *Save top tier for bride.* b *Cut 5" circle in center of second tier and slice as shown. Cut inner circle into 4 or 6 pieces.* c *Cut circle about 2½" in from edge. Slice as shown. Repeat for inner circle.* d *Make 16 servings from sheet cake 10" square.* e *A two-layer cake up to 9" in diameter can be cut into 8 servings; up to 11" in diameter, 16 servings.* f *40 servings from 12" cake.* g *32 servings from two-layer cake 9" x 13" (cut on solid verticals and broken horizontals); 64 servings from 12" x 17½" (cut on all lines). For clean cuts, dip knife into hot water or wipe off with damp sponge.*

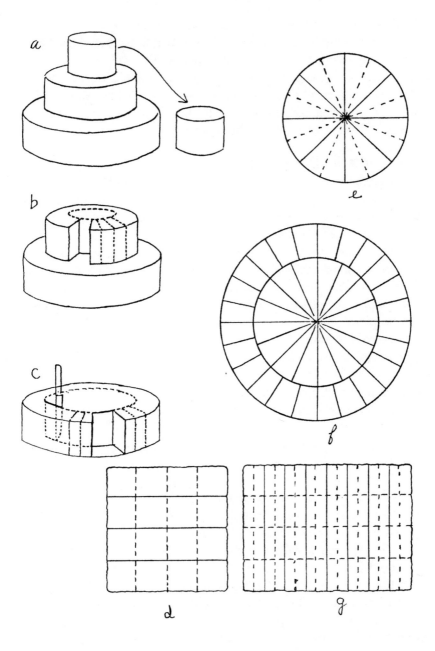

age. Have plenty of overall frosting ready; it will take three to four batches to frost and decorate a cake that will serve one hundred people. Plan to have the cake finished at least a full day before it is to be served, especially if it is to be transported any distance (see index for advice on transporting cake). There is less chance of the tiers slipping if the cake is not moved too soon after it is assembled. This will also give you time to be completely relaxed to receive the compliments that are sure to be forthcoming.

Separators in Tier Cakes

I prefer to assemble tier cakes without separators, because I feel the design has more continuity when the tiers are set one on the other in graduated sizes. But for those who wish to use separators, the following information will be helpful.

Separators are available in varied materials, styles and prices. The most widely used—plastic—consist of two plates, four dowels and four posts. The posts may be shaped like Grecian columns, swans, cornucopias or lattices. All posts have sockets which fit the knobs on the plates so they may be used interchangeably. Grecian columns are shown in figures 25c, 25d but the same method of assembly would apply to all other posts.

Start by assembling the lowest tier and work your way up. Insert dowels into each tier of cake.

Notice the ridges around the base of the knobs in the lower plate A. These provide a tight connection of the post for more stability. The ridges are absent on the knobs on the upper plate B, allowing the tier to be lifted off easily for transporting or serving.

The safest way to carry a tier cake which has separators is to disassemble it and carry it as individual cakes. It can easily be reassembled. To keep the cake from being damaged in transit you can prepare a styrofoam cradle for each tier (figure 31).

To assemble a cake using separators, frost as usual and insert dowels. Choose a separator at least 4" smaller than the cake below it and the same size or slightly larger than the cake above. For example, if the lower tier is 14" and the next is 9" or 10", you would use a 10" separator plate. (Separator plates in this type are available only in even numbers.) Center the lower plate A on the frosted tier with the knobs pointed upward as shown. Snap the four posts into place over the

Fig. 27. Doll Cake. a *Cake baked in a bowl set on a single layer of cake with filling between. Cut hole into cake if it was baked without central core.* b *Doll dropped into hole to* ½" *below her waist. Broken lines indicate frosting added to taper waist.* c *Bodice and skirt covered with frosting. Grooves in skirt are made with tines of a large meat fork (grooves* ¼" *to* ⅜" *apart) used as guide in piping ruffles.* d *Completed cake with ruffled skirt.*

knobs. Spread a small amount of frosting on the center of the upper plate to hold the cake securely. Center the tier on the upper plate B, the knobs pointed downward as shown Completely frost the cake, then put into place by easing the knobs into the sockets at the top of the posts. After all the tiers are in place as described previously the cake may be decorated as usual. The bottom borders may be left off each tier that is on a separator and added at the site. If this is not practical or possible use extra care in handling the tiers as there will be little if any space around the bottom of each plate once the border is in place.

Doll Cakes

Perfect for showers, engagement parties, etc.

Bake a cake in an 8″ ovenproof bowl and one in a layer cake pan of the same diameter as the bowl. Put the layer of cake on the prepared plate or base. Spread top with frosting or filling. Place bowl cake, flat side down, over filling. If top of bowl cake is not level, cut a piece off before placing on top of other cake. Cut a hole in the center of the cake deep enough to drop an 8″ doll into to ½″ below her waist. Cut the hole only wide enough for the doll to fit into tightly.

Paint the bodice on, using frosting and a watercolor brush, shaping the neckline and sleeves as desired. Frost the cake part (skirt) with the same frosting as the bodice. Apply frosting generously, then run the tip of a small icing spatula over it in an up and down motion to create the illusion of folds in the skirt. Pipe a shell border around the bottom of the skirt using the same frosting and a No. 30 tube.

Finish the cake using your own design or duplicate one of those illustrated.

Chapter 10

PARTY-FOOD DECORATIONS

Now that you have learned the basic steps in Cake Decorating, has it occurred to you how many other uses there are for a pastry bag and tips? Any substance which has been worked to the proper consistency can be squeezed through a bag and tips. Mashed potatoes, Cream Cheese, Old English Cheese, whipped cream and cookie dough are just a few.

I once knew a man whose hobby was making lovely ceramic pieces. A cake decorator by profession, he ran clay through a bag to make flowers, birds, etc. to trim his ceramic pieces; so you see, the possibilities are many. In this section I bring you some examples of these uses. I am sure you will discover others for yourself.

Cream Cheese Decorating

Cream cheese should be at room temperature. Place it in mixing bowl and beat until creamy. Add and beat in 3 tablespoons of milk or cream for each 8 ounces of cream cheese. This will give the proper consistency for spreading and most tube work. When cream cheese is to be used for making large roses (tube No. 126) it should be beaten without adding any milk or cream.

Sandwich loaf

Use day old unsliced Pullman or Sandwich loaves. Remove the top and bottom crusts, then slice lengthwise into slices ⅝" thick, remove the crusts from four slices. The remaining slices may be used for canapes or open face sandwiches.

Prepare a large serving tray or a double thickness of corrugated cardboard longer and wider than the loaf. Tape the cardboards together and cover with aluminum foil and doilies. Be certain that the channels in the cardboard run lengthwise or it may bend when the loaf is picked up.

Have filling prepared and chilled. Butter or margarine should be soft. Place three 8-ounce packages of cream cheese in mixing bowl and prepare as described above. Attach a No. 16 tube to a decorating bag and fill with cream cheese.

Place first slice of bread on tray and spread with butter. Pipe a line of cream cheese around the edge of the slice of bread. (This will prevent the filling from oozing out between the slices.) Spread ⅓ of the filling inside the cream cheese line. Top with a slice of bread which has been spread with butter on both sides. Repeat the above procedure until you have used four slices of bread and all the filling. *Do not* butter the top of the last slice of bread. Check to be sure the slices are stacked evenly. Dampen a piece of cheese cloth or a piece of paper towel and cover the top and sides of the loaf. Wrap the entire loaf in waxed paper or plastic wrap and refrigerate for about three hours.

To finish the loaf, frost top and sides smoothly with prepared cream cheese, reserving some for borders and decorations. The border may be white or colored. Tint the remaining cream cheese and decorate the top of the loaf as desired or duplicate one of the designs illustrated.

Any sandwich filling may be used in sandwich loaves. My guests have always enjoyed the Turkey Salad made from the recipe below.

Turkey salad sandwich filling

6 cups cooked turkey, diced (preferably white meat)
1 pint French Dressing
3 cups celery, finely chopped

6 hard-cooked eggs, mashed
1½ cups mayonnaise, chilled
½ cup sweet pickles, finely chopped

Remove skin and fat from turkey before dicing. Pack firmly into cup to measure. Place in bowl and pour French Dressing over all. Cover tightly and place in refrigerator to marinate for about 4 hours. Stir 4 or 5 times during this time to be sure all pieces of turkey become coated with marinade. Drain off any excess French Dressing, add remaining ingredients and mix well. Chill filling about 1 hour before using.

This recipe is sufficient for a three-pound loaf of bread which is approximately 18″ long and will serve 18 to 20. For smaller loaves, cut the recipe down proportionately.

Doll loaf

A beautiful edible centerpiece can be made from a round unsliced loaf of bread. Rye, pumpernickel, whole wheat, or Italian bread may be used. Prepare as described for regular sandwich loaf, only use all the slices of bread from the loaf. Before refrigerating, cut a small hole in the center. The hole should be deep enough to allow an eight inch doll to be dropped into it to about one half inch below her waist. It would, of course, be wide enough to slip the lower part of the doll's body into. Remove the doll, wrap and chill the loaf.

To complete the centerpiece, wrap the lower part of the doll's body in plastic cling wrap and insert into hole in center of the loaf. If the doll does not fit snuggly, stuff a few small pieces of bread down into the hole to help hold it in place. Frost and decorate the loaf as you would a doll cake using cream cheese instead of frosting. See complete decorating instructions with illustration (fig. 27).

Decorated Salad and Sandwich Bar (Fig. 28)

1. Candle Salad

Lay 1 slice pineapple on plate. Halve a banana crosswise and press upright into hole in pineapple, cut side down. Make handle by fastening ¼ slice of pineapple to it as shown using half a toothpick. Stick maraschino cherry on toothpick and insert in tip of banana for flame. Fill decorating bag with whipped cream or cream cheese; attach No. 16 tube. Use to pipe droplets down the side of the banana to simulate melting wax. Note: If salads are prepared more than half an hour before serving, brush bananas with lemon juice to prevent discoloration.

2. Tulip Salad

Use a 5″ length of celery stalk for the stem; two small leaves Romaine lettuce for leaves. Cut about ⅓ from the top of a firm plum tomato. Place remaining ⅔ on plate, cut side up, and bottom at tip of celery stalk. Press level teaspoonfuls of pink or yellow cream cheese around tomato for petals or pipe them on using tube No. 126. Carefully cover cut surface of tomato with black caviar for pollen.

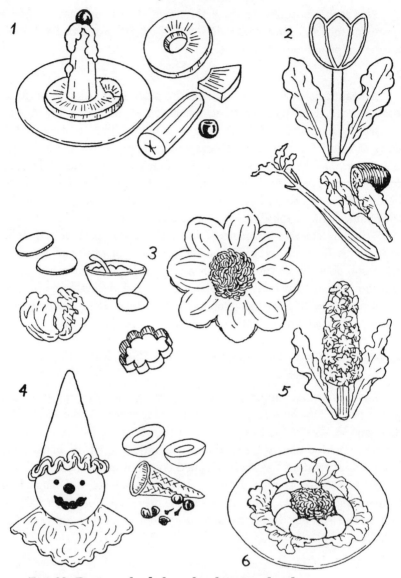

Fig. 28. *Decorated salads and a daisy sandwich.*

3. Daisy Sandwich

Cut 3 crosswise slices from a round loaf of bread (Italian, rye, or pumpernickel), about ⅝″ thick. Remove crusts. Spread with butter, then with meat, fish or egg salad. Cut outline to resemble 8 petals. Frost with cream cheese. Make pollen in center with sieved hard-cooked egg yolks. Serve on a bed of lettuce leaves. Cut into wedges to serve.

4. Clown Face Salad

Use a canned peach half, round side up, for the face. Cut about 4″ from the pointed end of a sugar ice cream cone. Frost with pastel-colored creamy cream cheese or stabilized whipped cream (see recipe on p. 154); use for hat. Fill decorating bag with cream cheese or whipped cream. Pipe a No. 30 zigzag where the hat meets the head. Change to No. 104 and pipe a ruffle around the neck. Make features of piping gel or use cloves for eyes and maraschino cherry pieces for the nose and mouth.

5. Hyacinth Salad

Use a half banana cut crosswise, a pineapple spear or a piece of cucumber cut first lengthwise, then crosswise. Place on a plate with a 3″ piece of celery stalk for a stem and two or three small Romaine lettuce leaves. Cover the piece of banana, pineapple or cucumber with No. 30 flat stars of pink, yellow, light blue or pale violet cream cheese.

6. Waterlily Salad

Use lettuce leaves for lily pads. Cut a thin slice from top and bottom of a firm tomato. Form petals around tomato with a No. 126 tube or a demi-tasse or baby feeding spoon, and white or very pale pink cream cheese. Make pollen in center from sieved hard-cooked egg yolks. For a particularly striking effect serve on a blue plate or line plate with blue cellophane before arranging salad on it.

Holiday Bar (Fig. 29)

1. Santa Claus Face Salad

Use a canned pear half, round side up. Brush the round part with pink piping gel for face. Brush the elongated part with red gel for

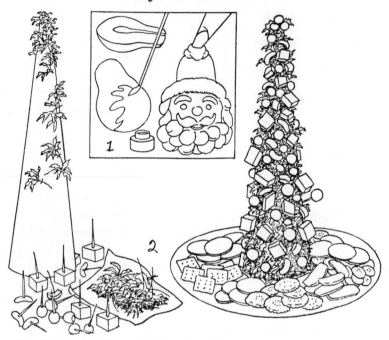

Fig. 29. Santa Claus Salad and Tidbit Tree.

the hat. Use blue gel for eyes and red gel for the nose and mouth. Pipe eyebrows and mustache with No. 4 using whipped cream or cream cheese. Change to No. 30 tube. Pipe the beard and the fur trim on the hat.

2. Tidbit Tree

Cover a 12″ styrofoam cone with parsley by stapling into place. Fasten ¾″ cubes of ham, cheese, pineapple to the cone with toothpicks. Tiny pickles or pickle slices and stuffed olives may also be added. Place cone in the center of a large serving plate. Surround with crackers, slices of party rye bread and melba toast pieces.

Gelatin Desserts and Fruit Aspics

Stabilized whipped cream

To garnish or decorate with whipped cream several hours before serving it will be necessary to stabilize the cream first. This can be done by one of the following methods.

1. Soften 1 teaspoon unflavored gelatin in 4 teaspoons cold water

for 5 minutes. Place over hot water to dissolve. Beat ½ pint heavy cream until it begins to thicken. Pour the gelatin mixture into the cream in a very thin stream while stirring to blend. Add 2 tablespoons confectioners' sugar and beat until the cream is stiff enough to retain swirls. *Do not overbeat.*

2. Use piping gel according to the directions on the can.

3. Use All-Purpose Stabilizer (see Sources of Supply) according to the package directions.

I have found the last two methods superior to the first as far as simplicity of use and holding power.

Molded vegetable salads and aspics

Use cream cheese as described previously or decorate using a mixture of 1 part mayonnaise and 2 parts cream cheese. Cream cheese mixed with mayonnaise should not be thinned with milk or cream.

Chapter 11

DECORATING FUN FOR CHILDREN

Gumdrop Flowers

Use a rolling pin to flatten the gumdrops, sprinkling the work surface with granulated sugar to prevent sticking.

Tulip

Roll a large red, yellow or pink gumdrop into an oval. Cut the oval in half across the short way. Using the round part as the bottom, snip two small "V" shaped pieces out of the top with the points of a scissors, forming three petals. Use green string-type jelly candies for stems, cutting them lengthwise. Flatten two other green string-shaped candies and press next to stem for tulip leaves.

Daisy

Roll a large white or yellow gumdrop round and quite flat. Slash around the edge in eight places, cutting almost to the center. To form petals, spread cut pieces apart and pinch end of each to form a point. Use a thin slice of a small yellow or black gumdrop for the center. Use yellow on the white daisy and black for the yellow one.

Rose

Roll large pink, yellow or white gumdrops into an oval. Cut ovals in half across the short way. Roll one half oval, round side up, and pinch together to form a bud. Roll three more gumdrops into ovals and cut in half. Stretch and shape the seven half ovals to form petals.

Stick petals around the bud, overlapping them and shaping them further, if necesary. Leaves may be cut from flattened green gumdrops or green jelly candy leaves may be used.

Marshmallow Candy Characters (Color Plate 2)

Teddy bear

For each bear you will need 2 large marshmallows, 12 whole, and one half miniature marshmallows.

The large marshmallows used are the kind packed in boxes; the puffed ones are too soft.

1. Fasten the two large marshmallows together with toothpicks so they look like a figure 8.

2. String 2 miniature marshmallows with the flat sides together on a toothpick for each arm. Fasten by pressing exposed part of pick into body in proper place on each side.

3. String three small marshmallows on a toothpick for each leg. Fasten to the body by sticking exposed pick in at proper place.

4. Make ears by placing a small marshmallow, flat side forward, on a half toothpick. Press point of pick into head to fasten.

5. Cut a small marshmallow in half, keeping the flat side up. Press into position for nose. Moisten cut edge slightly if you have trouble getting the nose to stick.

Cowboy

1. Fasten two large marshmallows together to form a figure 8.

2. Split a large marshmallow to within ¼″ of the top. Spread bottom apart for legs, and fasten to bottom of figure 8.

3. Snip about ⅓ from a large marshmallow, then cut piece in two for feet. Attach to legs with small pieces of toothpick.

4. String 1½ small marshmallows on toothpicks for arms.

5. Cut a thin slice from the flat side of a large marshmallow and elongate to a slightly oval shape for the hat brim.

6. Stretch the ⅔ marshmallow left from the feet to the proper shape for the crown of the hat. Stick to the brim, cut side down.

7. Place hat on head and fasten in place with a piece of toothpick.

8. Paint facial features with paste color applied with a fine brush or pipe on with icing from a parchment cone.

Snowman

1. Fasten two large marshmallows together to form a figure 8.

2. Use toothpicks to attach arms and legs—half a small marshmallow for each arm, and two for each leg.

3. Make a hat with a small slice from a large marshmallow for the brim and a small marshmallow as the crown.

4. Paint on features and buttons as described above for the cowboy.

Sitting rabbit

1. Cut a large marshmallow in half and squeeze together to round off for a head.

2. Fasten to a whole large marshmallow body.

3. Snip half marshmallow left from the head in two lengthwise; stretch slightly to form long ears. Fasten to head with pieces of toothpick.

4. Stick a small marshmallow, flat side forward, to each side for arms. Point arms and legs forward, rather than sticking out from the sides.

5. Flatten bottom of body, pointing forward.

6. Facial features may be painted on or rabbit may be used plain. A bit of pink may be painted at the front of each ear.

Ice Cream Cone Cornucopia

Spread a coat of strawcolored Decorator Frosting (yellow mixed with a bit of brown) over the outside of a sugar cone. (Do not use a waffle cone as it becomes soft when it comes into contact with moisture from the frosting.) Pipe basket weave design over the outside of the cone using the strawcolored frosting and No. 6 and No. 48 tubes. Then finish the open end with a shell or rope border using tube No. 16 and strawcolored frosting.

A very young child can make the cornucopia too. Spread with a thick coat of frosting and then score in wiggly lines with the tines of a fork. It will be helpful if the fork is dipped into hot water from time to time.

For easier handling, allow the cornucopia to dry for a day before using. Place it on a cake at an attractive angle and arrange molded fondant fruit spilling from it.

Ice Cream Cone Christmas Tree

Frost a sugar cone generously with dark green Decorator Frosting. While the frosting is still moist roll the cone in coarse green sugar. Stand the tree upright and decorate with dots of colored frosting and colored candy balls (silver and gold dragees). The dragees are best applied using a tweezer. Two small gummed foil stars may be pasted together foil side out and placed at the top of the tree. Hold in place with a dab of frosting if you have difficulty getting it to stick.

Molding Fruit from Fondant

The following sizes are scaled to fit a cornucopia made from an ice cream cone. Fruit may be molded into larger pieces, if desired, keeping the sizes of the fruit in correct proportion to each other.

Dust the table or board with sifted confectioners' sugar or cornstarch to prevent sticking. If the fondant seems very soft, knead in some extra confectioners' sugar before attempting to mold any fruit.

Fondant for modelling

⅓ cup soft butter or margarine
¼ cup light corn syrup
½ teaspoon salt

1 pound sifted confectioners' sugar (about 4 cups)
1 teaspoon flavoring

Blend butter, corn syrup, salt, and flavoring in a large bowl. Add sifted confectioners' sugar all at once. Mix first with a spoon and then with the hands, kneading in the dry sugar. Turn out on table or board which has been dusted with confectioners' sugar and continue to knead until mixture is well blended and smooth. Shape and color as desired.

Apply paste color to each piece of fondant using a toothpick. Then knead it until the color is evenly distributed.

Mix a batch of fondant and divide into five pieces. Break off about ¼ of one of the pieces, and color it purple. Color the remaining ¾ bright orange. Set the colored pieces aside and cover with plastic wrap while you color the remaining pieces. Color two of the other pieces yellow, one green, and one red. Set aside and cover with plastic wrap to prevent crusting over.

For maximum ease in arranging the fruit, allow to dry thoroughly. All the molding may be done well in advance as the fondant will last a month or more without any appreciable loss of flavor. Store

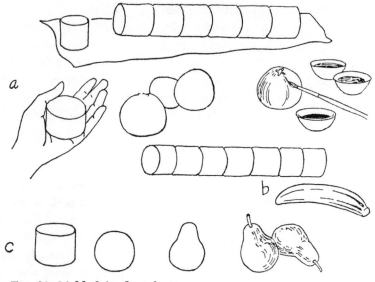

Fig. 30. Molded fondant fruit.

molded fruit at room temperature in a covered box or container until needed.

Bananas

Roll one half piece of yellow fondant into a rope about ¼" thick. Cut into pieces about 1½" long. Curve the pieces slightly and pinch the ends to resemble the tips of bananas. Dry finished pieces on a cookie sheet covered with wax paper. When dried, touch up with brown paste color applied with a watercolor brush. Remove excess color with a small piece of cleansing tissue wrapped around a toothpick.

Grapefruit

Roll ¾ piece of yellow fondant into a rope about ¾" thick. Cut into pieces ¾" long. Roll into balls. Press a small hole into center of the top with a toothpick which has been dipped in brown color.

Lemons

From ¼ piece of yellow fondant roll rope ¼" thick and cut into pieces ½" long. Roll into balls, then elongate, tapering end to resemble shape of lemon.

Apples

Use red or green fondant. A few of each add variety to the assortment of fruit. Roll colored fondant into rope ⅝" thick. Cut into pieces ⅝" long and roll into balls. Elongate some of the balls to resemble the shape of the Delicious apple. Others may be left round. Press indentation in the top with a toothpick. A piece of chocolate shot may be inserted into the hole for a stem if desired. A blush may be painted on the green apples in the same manner as was done on the peaches.

Grapes

Use purple or green fondant. A bunch of each color is attractive in a fruit arrangement. Pull off tiny bits of fondant and roll into balls less than ⅛" in diameter. Cut a small, slightly triangular piece of wafer paper for each bunch of grapes. Beginning at the bottom point of the wafer triangle, build the cluster of grapes. It should, of course, be thicker at the top; have more layers at the top. Add a few extra grapes here and there to make the bunches more lifelike. If you have difficulty getting the grapes to stick to each other or the wafer paper, moisten them slightly with a bit of water.

Plums

Plums may be made from any remaining purple fondant. Cut into pieces the same size as for lemons. Shape into small ovals. Make cleft in them as for peaches. Let dry.

Peaches

Add a bit of red fondant to one-half piece of yellow fondant and blend to attain peach color. Roll pieces of fondant into a rope about ⅝" thick. Cut into pieces about ⅝" long. Roll each piece into a ball. Make a cleft in one side with the dull edge of a table knife or a flat toothpick. Allow to dry slightly, then paint red blush on one side with red paste color and brush. Blend color and remove excess with piece of cleansing tissue on toothpick. Press a small depression in the stem end with a toothpick which has first been dipped into brown paste color.

Oranges

Roll and cut orange fondant the same as for apples, eliminating the blush or elongating the balls. Mark stem end with a small indentation made with a toothpick.

Pears

Roll and cut green fondant the same size as for oranges. After rolling pieces into a ball, elongate the top part slightly by rolling between the fingertips. A blush may be painted on as described previously.

Sugar Molding

Of the many facets of decorating, sugar molding is one of the most rewarding and is easy enough for even the youngest member of the family to do.

The variety of molds available is almost endless. They range from very tiny ones, holding about 1 teaspoonful of sugar, to very large pieces such as a Cinderella's coach. The method is always the same regardless of the size.

Mix granulated sugar with just enough water to dampen it sufficiently so it can be packed tightly into the molds with no loss of shape when it is turned out. It is very similar to the way sand is packed into a pail and then turned out at the beach.

With experience you will learn to judge by the feel of the sugar when it is damp enough. Until you do, mix on the basis of 2 cups of sugar and one tablespoon of cold water. Mix by rubbing between the hands until all the sugar is uniformly dampened. If the sugar is to be colored, add the color to the water to dissolve it, then mix into sugar.

Cut pieces of corrugated cardboard larger than the mold. Pack the sugar tightly into the mold, especially in areas such as faces where clear detail is important. Level off top with a straight-edged knife. Place cardboard over the mold, invert the two, and lift the mold straight up to remove. If the sugar sticks in the mold, it was too wet. If the piece crumbles, the sugar was too dry. Add extra water or dry sugar to correct the problem.

The molded pieces are left undisturbed until they dry. They may be used as they are, or painted and decorated using Royal Icing.

Panorama eggs

Pack the sugar firmly into both halves of the molds as described above. Before setting aside to dry, cut a portion of sugar out of the pointed ends of both halves with a tablespoon. Prop a piece of wax paper securely against the cut part to keep it from crusting. Allow the exposed parts to dry until a hard crust forms on the surface. In dry weather, about an hour is sufficient for a large egg. Smaller ones will dry faster. After they have dried, carefully lift each half and hollow it with a teaspoon, leaving a shell of sugar about ¼" thick. Allow to dry again until the inside surface is hard and dry. The inside of the bottom may be painted with green Royal Icing, but be careful not to use so much as to soak the shell. Then arrange the scene inside. Flowers, chicks, rabbits, eggs, etc. may be used. Paint the inside of the top shell blue, starting at the center and painting the back half only. Painting the entire top does not allow enough light inside the egg. Press a line of Royal Icing around the top edges of the bottom half and put top half over it. The icing will hold the two together. Cut a piece of cellophane large enough to cover the peephole. Pipe a line of icing around the edge of the hole and press the cellophane into place.

Using either a No. 16 or No. 30 tube, pipe a border all around the outside of the egg to cover the seam. Pipe a border around the peephole.

Decorate the top of the egg with a spray of small flowers or chicks, rabbits, etc. A greeting or a name may also be piped on.

Chapter 12

DECORATED CAKES FOR PROFIT

If you bake well and enjoy doing it, you might consider starting a small "pin-money" project. This sort of endeavor can be quite successful but you must be sure to consider the following points before starting.

Pricing Cakes

You will work slowly, at first, and will have difficulty deciding what to charge. A good rule of thumb is to multiply by three the price of all ingredients and materials. Be certain to include all expenses—cake circles, doilies, boxes, etc. Keep your orders neatly recorded in a special notebook, and make a cross reference on your calendar several days ahead of the expected delivery date.

Keep yourself and your home spotless and organized; your customers are sure to notice.

Do not agree to bake and decorate for only the cost of the ingredients. Once started this is a difficult practice to get away from. Donate the cake outright rather than give the impression that by paying for ingredients the customer has virtually paid for the cake. You have a right to expect adequate compensation.

Check local ordinances to be certain there are no legal obstacles.

Publicizing Your Services

Notify caterers and even florists in your area of your service.

Place a few ads in local newspapers. Personals are usually inexpensive and get a high rate of readership.

164

1. Locomotive Cake.

2. Jack-o-lantern Cake.

3. Baby's First Birthday Cake.

4. Happy Clowns Birthday Cake.

5. Bassinet Cake; Baby Sweater Set.

6. Bar Mitzvah Cake.

7. French Poodle Birthday Cake.

8. Sweet Sixteen Cake.

9. Cascade-of-Chrysanthemums Cake.

10. Pansy Birthday Cake; Daffodil Birthday Cake.

11. Vase of Roses Cake; Double Bell Cake.

12. Flag Cake; First Class Male Cake.

13. Sports Cakes: Golf and Basketball.

14. Crown Cake for Father's Day.

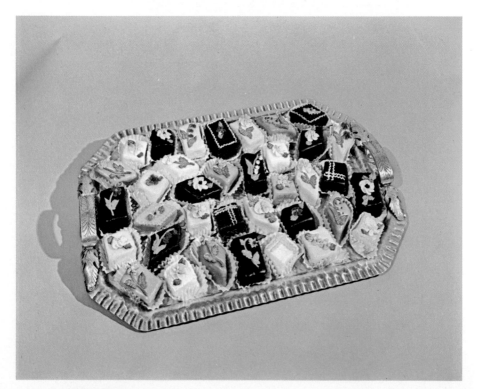

15. Petits Fours.

16. Thanksgiving Cakes:
Chrysanthemum and Cornucopia.

17. Poinsettia Christmas Cake.

18. Party Cookies.

19. Shamrock Cake; Confirmation Cake.

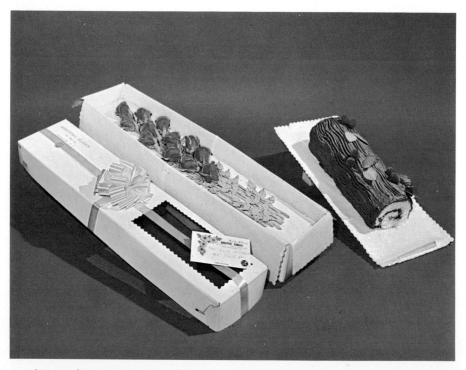

20. Washington Log; Box of Roses.

21. Easter Hat and Purse Set.

22. Lamb Cake; Bunny Cake.

23. Easter Egg Cake.

24. Easter Cross Cake.

25. Panorama Eggs; Sugar-Molded Ducks.

26. Wedding Cake trimmed with fresh flowers.

27. Bridal Shower Cake; Mortarboard Cake.

28. Doll Cakes.

29. Pink Wedding Cake.

30. Daisy Wedding Cake.

31. Engagement Cake.

32. Ice Cream Bombe.

33. Dessert Buffet.

34. Sandwich Loaves.

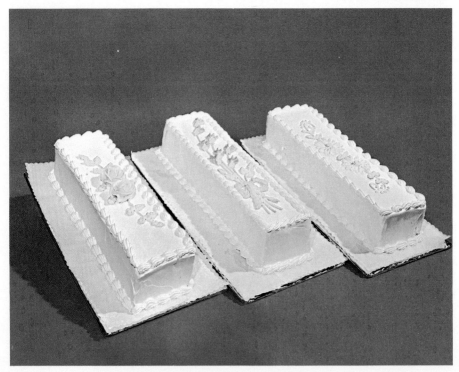

A note to the family of the engaged girl (see announcements in local papers) might result in orders for wedding or shower cakes (enclose recommendations from a few satisfied customers). Be sure to mention that you can coordinate the design of the cake with the floral decoration (bride's bouquet, corsage, table centerpiece etc.)

Call program chairmen of local clubs offering to give a cake decorating demonstration for their organization. You should expect to be paid a fee, or to be reimbursed for expenses.

Local businessmen might like personalized cakes for anniversaries, holidays, service award parties, etc.

Let the word get around through friends and relatives that you are willing to take orders for decorated cakes.

Enter cakes at local fairs and baking contests.

Donate a cake here and there (cake sale at the P.T.A., church bazaar, etc.). This will make people aware of your talents and is inexpensive advertising. The gift of a cake to a local woman's page editor with a short news release about your personal service could also reach many potential customers.

About the cakes themselves, do not skimp on quality ingredients. A high-quality cake is bound to cost a bit more, but most people are willing to pay for a superior product. Give your customers beautifully decorated and delicious cakes and you will have an unbeatable combination . . . with lots of word-of-mouth advertising.

Cakes and Cookies for the Bazaar

A cake and cookie booth at a Fair or Bazaar is an excellent way to raise funds for your church or club.

The first step is to appoint a chairman, a willing worker with time to devote and a genuine interest in the job. The entire project will require patience, diplomacy and persuasiveness on her part. It will be up to the chairman to find the right person for each job. A good committee is made up of people with diversified talents but a single goal: to make the booth profitable. Mrs. Jones may not be much of a baker but if she has a way with people she will be invaluable as a sales person. If Mrs. Smith has a flair for packaging and displaying things attractively she can also be a great help. Not too many people will come forward but few will refuse if approached in the right manner.

There is little doubt that because of your talent for baking and decorating you may be asked to serve on such a committee or at least contribute some of your decorated cakes and cookies.

It has been my experience that large, elaborately decorated cakes do not bring a good price if offered for sale. More profit can be realized if the cake is used as a prize in a raffle or a contest. However, small (not over 10″) cakes, simply decorated, will sell well. At holiday time, cakes decorated with appropriate designs and inscriptions may be featured. If cakes are decorated for general use or occasions it is best to leave the inscriptions off. Have a committee member with a knowledge of decorating on hand, to add suitable inscriptions as the cakes are sold. This can be done quickly and easily by having small cones of piping gel in various colors on hand. Personalizing cakes makes them more salable and at a better price.

If space for a few tables and chairs is available, cake can be sold by the slice with coffee, tea or hot chocolate and, in warm weather, cold drinks.

Plain cakes or cakes with just the tops frosted are also popular. Bake them in disposable aluminum foil pans, wrap in plastic film or colored cellophane and tie with ribbons. This type of packaging is attractive and comparatively inexpensive.

Cookies are a favorite of young and old alike and always very salable. They may be packed in an almost endless variety of ways. Cookie-filled toy trucks, carts and baskets are sure to attract the younger set and their grandmothers too. After the toy is filled with cookies, wrap the entire thing in cellophane or plastic film. The price should reflect the cost of the toy as well as the cookies. Ask local merchants to donate the toys and the profit will be even greater. Inexpensive household items also make novel containers. Try filling dustpans, goblets, plastic bowls and plates or apothecary jars (some instant coffees are packed in them). Wrap in cellophane or plastic film, and tie with ribbon. Coffee cans can be covered with adhesive-backed plastic in gay designs and used as cookie cannisters. Plastic lids may be left plain or painted with brightly colored enamel.

The ideas suggested are just some of the possibilities; there are many others. Keep packages inexpensive but attractive. Eye appeal is half of taste appeal. *One final word of advice*: Be certain all items offered for sale are the finest. Do not offer poor quality items and expect to sell them in the name of Sweet Charity.

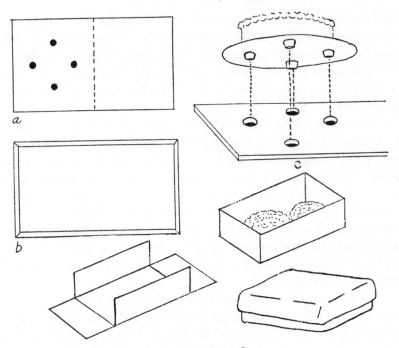

Fig. 31. Cradle for transporting tier cakes.

How to Transport Cakes

A cake of average size presents few problems when it must be carried to a bazaar, demonstration, reception, etc. Cake boxes afford all the protection needed if you observe a few simple precautions. The plate or corrugated cardboard base should be at least 2″ larger than the cake to keep it from hitting the sides of the box. If the cake box is to be placed on a car seat, roll a newspaper or magazine tightly and press it into the back part of the seat where it slopes back. The rolled paper should bring this part of the seat up to the level of the front edge. Place the cake with one edge of the box on the roll and it should be quite level. This will eliminate the possibility of the cake sliding back on the plate or base inside the box.

Very large or tall cakes may be placed in corrugated cartons. Choose a carton as close to the size of the base or plate as possible for a snug fit. Using a sharp knife or razor blade, cut down through two corners of the carton on one side and bring the side out flat. Slide the cake in and tape the side back into place. To remove the cake easily, cut the tape and lower the side of the carton. This will eliminate the need to lift the cake in or out of the carton. A cover may be made for the carton from a large piece of aluminum foil.

Tier cakes are most easily transported in the back of a station wagon but may also be carried in the trunk of a car (check heights to be sure).

Use a blanket to cushion the cake against bumps and prevent it from slipping, as it might on a hard surface. Avoid excessive speed and quick stops. It is a good idea to have some extra icing and flowers or decorations with you in case repairs are needed when you arrive. Also bring along the decorating tips you used on the cake and a pastry bag or parchment paper. You'll probably have no need for any of these, but take them for your peace of mind. *Never* transport a cake with the top ornament in place as they are usually topheavy and could easily fall and damage the cake. Put the ornament in place when the cake is on the table.

To transport tier cakes on separators prepare cradles as follows *before decorating the cake.* Trace around the knobs on the lower plate after placing it on a sheet of ½" styrofoam. Center the plate so there will be at least 1" margin between it and the edges of the styrofoam sheet. Cut the styrofoam out of the traced circles. (see figure 31a) Place each piece of styrofoam on a cookie sheet with sides or a jelly roll pan.

After the cake is decorated lift the top plates holding the cake and drop the feet into the prepared cradle. (see figure 31c). Each tier may then be placed in a box if desired.

To remove the tiers from the cradle slide the fingertips between the separator plate and the top of the styrofoam sheet (there will be about ¼" space between them) and lift the tier straight up. This will remove the knobs at the bottom of the separators from the holes in the styrofoam. The cake is now ready to be reassembled.

Chapter 13

FIFTY CELEBRATION CAKES AND PARTY FOODS

Advance Preparation

Frosting flowers

Frosting flowers made on wax paper should be allowed to dry at least 24 hours; longer for dark colors. If time is short, you can harden thick flowers such as roses, chrysanthemums, etc. in the freezer or refrigerator for 12-15 minutes. Do not allow them to freeze, as they become sticky and soft when thawed. Do not use the shortcut drying method on thin flowers (drop flowers, pansies, daisies, etc.) as the breakage would be tremendous.

Air drying is a far more satisfactory method of drying flowers. Therefor, in the instructions which follow, air drying is specified. Set the frosting flowers on a cookie sheet as you make them, and let air dry for the time indicated. For long-time storage of frosting flowers, set them in a covered box one layer deep. The flowers will last for months but the flavor extract fades after a week or two.

To remove flowers from wax paper squares, peel away paper or slide the end of a thin spatula under them and lift off. The same method may be used whether the flowers are chilled or air dried.

Cakes

See Chapter 1 for full instructions on how to freeze baked cakes before and after frosting. Leftover decorated cakes can be refrigerated after the party or frozen in a cake box for a month or so. Cakes with custard-type fillings should not be frozen; they are perishable and should be kept refrigerated between serving times.

Locomotive Cake

Color plate 1 • You will need:
   1 large loaf cake (2 recipes Old-Fashioned Pound Cake)
   1 recipe Chocolate Buttercream
   6 cardboard circles—four 2" and two 2¾"
   1 cup White Whipped Buttercream, colored yellow
   1   3" x 3½" piece of lightweight cardboard
   1 piece aluminum foil same size as cardboard above
   1 1" bell and sandwich pick to hold it
   yellow birthday candles and holders
   about 30 large candy pebbles (available in candy shops)
   14" x 18" tray or foil-covered cardboard
   black jelly beans
   1½ cups coconut, colored green

Day before

1. Preheat oven to 300° F. Grease and flour 15" x 4" x 4" loaf pan. Prepare batter for Old-Fashioned Pound Cake. Pour into prepared pan and bake about 1 hour 55 minutes or until cake tests done. Cool in pan on rack 15 minutes. Turn out of pan and cool top side up on rack. Make frosting while cake is baking and cooling.

2. Place cold cake on center of tray or board *bottom side up*. Measure 5¾" from one end of cake. Make a slit about ¾" deep across cake at this point. Round the four corners of cake between the slit and end of cake to form engine.

3. Cut a slice ¾" thick from opposite end of cake. Lay slice on top of cake just past rounded part to form top of cab; cement into place with Buttercream.

4. Cut another slice of cake ⅜" from same end of cake. Cut in half crosswise, put one piece aside for nibbles. Cut other piece to a point on one long side. Cement to lower front of engine with frosting for cow catcher. The pointed part should be up.

5. Make a slit 1" deep in top of cake just beyond where the slice was added for cab. Make a diagonal slit 1" away from first, and have them meet at bottom. Remove wedge of cake, forming a separation between coal car and cab.

6. Frost entire cake with Chocolate Buttercream. Spread cardboard

circles with Chocolate Buttercream and press two small ones on each side of the engine for wheels. Use large ones on coal car.

7. Fill decorating bag with yellow Buttercream and attach a No. 16 tube. Use to trim locomotive and wheels as shown in color plate.

8. Make stack by rolling foil and cardboard together to form cylinder 3½″ high. Fasten with cellophane tape and press into frosting on engine.

9. Hook bell to top of sandwich pick, then press other end into cake to suspend bell.

10. Put candles on top of cab.

11. Pipe ties first, then tracks over them, to front and back of the locomotive, using tube No. 48, flat side up, and Chocolate Buttercream.

12. Fasten a row of candy pebbles on each side of tracks by first piping dabs of frosting on their undersides and then pressing into place.

13. Snip jelly beans into pieces with scissors. Pile on top of coal car.

14. Sprinkle area between candy pebbles and edges of board with green coconut.

NOTE: To color coconut mix a small amount of color with about 1 tablespoon water in a cookie sheet with sides or a sheet cake pan. Pour in about 12 ounces of coconut and toss with forks or the hands till uniformly colored. Spread out on cookie sheet to dry before using. For smaller quantities of coconut use less water and color.

TO SERVE: Remove the bell and the stack. Cut as any loaf cake into 14 to 16 slices.

Jack-o-lantern Cake

Color plate 2 • You will need:
   2 cakes baked in an 8″ or 9″ two-quart ovenproof bowl (2 recipes Old-Fashioned Pound Cake)
   1 recipe White Whipped Buttercream or 1½ recipes Creamy Frosting colored bright orange
   ¼ cup Chocolate Fudge, Chocolate Buttercream, or brown Decorator Frosting
   1 lollypop stick or sandwich pick
   2 green Jelly Candy leaves
   Removable angel cake core or 6-ounce frozen orange juice can

Day before

Preheat oven, prepare pan and removable core as recipe directs. If using orange juice can, cover smoothly with aluminum foil and fill with rice or dry beans to weight down. Mix, bake, and cool cakes as directed.

1. Level tops (flat sides of cakes) if necessary. Cut a thin slice from round part of one cake. Place this down on cake plate. Spread top with orange frosting. Place second cake, flat side down, over frosting to complete round shape.

2. Frost generously with orange Buttercream, then run tip of a small icing spatula up and down to make ridges.

3. Use a toothpick to draw the eyes, nose and mouth. Fill in with brown or chocolate frosting and a No. 6 tube.

3. String the two jelly leaves one over the other on the sandwich pick for the stem. Fasten by pressing the exposed part of the pick into cake.

TO SERVE: Cut tall thin slices or cut across first, then into 12. About 24 servings in all.

Baby's First Birthday Cake

Color plate 3. It's really two cakes, one for the little guests, the other for the grownups. • You will need:
   ½ recipe Royal Icing
   1 recipe White Cake (10" round)
   1 recipe Lemon Filling
   1 recipe White Whipped Buttercream
   ½ yard white Sasheen ribbon ½" wide
   ¼ cup blue piping gel
   ¼ cup green piping gel
   1 pink or blue 3" birthday candle

Several days ahead

As far in advance as convenient but at least three days before, prepare Royal Icing. Make 9 chicks and 2 rabbits on wax paper following directions under Figure Piping. (It's a good idea to make extra decorations for use another time; they keep indefinitely in the cake drawer.)

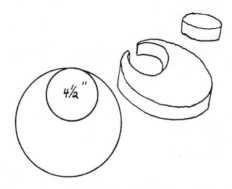

Fig. 32. Pattern for baby's first birthday cake.

Day before or early on the day

1. Bake cake. Make filling and Buttercream.

2. Using small plate as pattern, cut out a 4½" circle from cake (se fig. 32). Carefully remove this circle. Split both cakes and spread filling between layers.

3. Place cakes, top side up, on separate plates or doily covered boards.

4. Reserve 1½ cups white Buttercream for borders.

5. Color remaining frosting blue or pink and use to frost both cakes smoothly.

6. Cut ribbon in half and press one end of each piece into neck edge of bib for ties, ends resting on the plate.

7. Using tube 16, border both cakes with a zigzag (to stimulate rickrack) of white Buttercream.

8. Inscribe using tube No. 4 and blue piping gel.

9. Pipe lines and grass with green gel and a No. 2 tube. Press rabbits and chicks into place.

10. Pipe a large rosette of pink or blue Buttercream about 1" in from back edge of small cake using tube No. 30. Insert birthday candle into rosette.

TO SERVE: Cut small cake into 4 wedges, bib into about 10 slices.

Happy Clowns Birthday Cake

Color plate 4 • You will need:
  2 cake layers, 9" each (1 recipe Sour Milk Chocolate Cake)
  1 recipe Decorator Frosting
  1 recipe Buttercream Frosting No. 1
  ¼ cup red piping gel
  1 tablespoon each blue, green and yellow piping gel
  4 styrofoam balls (1" each)
  12" florist wire
  piece of aluminum foil 4" x 1"

Two days before

Mold 5 balls for heads from 2 tablespoons Decorator Frosting as directed under Figure Piping.

Day before

1. Bake cake as directed in recipe. Make Buttercream Frosting No. 1. Place cooled layer of cake on plate, bottom side up; spread with Buttercream. Top with second layer, again bottom side up. Frost top and sides smoothly with Buttercream.

2. Divide remaining Decorator Frosting into 4 parts. Remove about 2 tablespoons from each, making a fifth, and smaller, portion of frosting. Add few drops of water to this portion of frosting only; blend and set aside. Color larger portions as follows: 1 blue, 1 yellow, 1 pink and 1 green.

3. Pipe inscription with red piping gel and a No. 4 tube.

4. Pipe clowns in desired positions as explained under Figure Piping. Two are dressed in yellow and the others in each remaining color. The white, thinned frosting is used for ruffles on all clowns. These may be edged in different colors of piping gel.

5. Fill a small parchment cone with red piping gel and cut a small tip from it. Use to pipe on noses and mouths. Mix brown color into remaining white frosting, and use in a parchment cone with a small tip cut off, for eyes and hair. Cut tip larger and pipe on the shoes.

6. Pipe No. 30 shell border around cake and between clowns, using Buttercream or alternate-colored shells of Decorator Frosting left from making the clowns.

7. Cover each styrofoam ball with a different color piping gel. Cut florist wire into 4 equal pieces. Insert 1 end of each wire into a styrofoam ball and the other end through a clown's wrist and down into cake to hold it securely.

8. Fold aluminum foil in half and then in half again so that it resembles a folding mirror. Place in front of clown in center of cake.

Baby Sweater Set

Color plate 5 • You will need:
   Sweater set pattern (fig. 33)
   1 sheet cake 12" x 17¼" (1 recipe Butter Cake or 2 recipes Enriched Yellow Cake)
   14" x 18" corrugated cardboard covered with foil or doily
   1 recipe White Whipped Buttercream

Day before

Preheat oven to 325° F. Grease bottom of pan and line with wax paper. Mix batter and pour into prepared pan. Bake about 50 to 55 minutes or until cake tests done. Cool in pan on rack 10 to 15 minutes. Turn out of pan, remove paper from bottom and cool, top side up.

While cake is baking make frosting. Make paper or cardboard pattern. Lay patterns of sweater, hat, and booties on cooled cake and press straight pins through them into cake. Cut around pieces using a sharp knife. Remove patterns and pins. Transfer sweater cake to upper part of board.

DECORATE AS FOLLOWS:

1. Remove 1 cup Buttercream to small bowl, color light green.

2. Color remaining frosting yellow. Cover sweater with thin coat of yellow frosting. Place hat and booties on cookie sheet, leaving ample space between. Cover with coat of yellow frosting. Let cakes stand 1 hour to set crumbs; frost smoothly with Buttercream.

3. Using pin or toothpick, mark line ⅝" from neck edge of sweater and a straight line down front (see diagram).

4. Fill bag with green frosting and attach a No. 48 tube; fill second bag with yellow and attach a No. 6 tube.

5. Pipe short lines at neck edge as indicated by solid lines on diagram. Pipe a ribbon of green frosting over these lines with smooth side

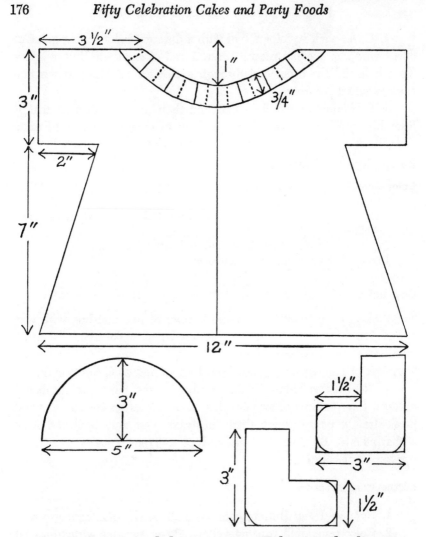

Fig. 33. Pattern for baby sweater set. Enlarge to the dimensions shown.

of tube up. Change to bag of yellow, and pipe lines over ribbon as indicated by broken lines in diagram.

6. Attach No. 16 tube to bag of yellow frosting and pipe a rope border at edge of neck and over the line 5⁄8″ from edge, covering ends of No. 6 lines. Cover left half of sweater with vertical rows of shells (same as shell border), keeping rows close together. Start

first row of shells at edge of left sleeve and continue across to within ⅛" from center line. Cover right half of sweater with shells, starting ⅛" to right of center line and continuing to edge of right sleeve.

7. Pipe a No. 16 yellow rope border to left of line at the center front (border should slightly overlap last row of shells) starting at neck edge and going down front and around bottom of cake. Pipe a matching border over right side of sweater also, having two borders meet at bottom.

8. With the bag of green frosting pipe a bow and streamers at neck as shown. Change to No. 30 and pipe a green rosette at end of each streamer.

TO FINISH HAT:

1. Still working on the cookie sheet, cover back and sides of hat with horizontal rows of shells using No. 16 tube and yellow Buttercream. *Do not cover* top or front. Carefully lift hat from cookie sheet with pancake turner and place on board below the sweater, leaving room for booties. Cover top of hat with vertical rows of shells.

2. Change to No. 104 on bag of green frosting and pipe a ruffle at front of hat. Border edge of hat with a yellow rope, same as sweater. Pipe green ties on hat using No. 48; add a rosette at end of each using No. 30.

BOOTIES:

1. Finish back of first bootie with horizontal rows of shells while it is still on cookie sheet, using No. 16 and yellow frosting. Transfer to cake board and finish bootie with rows of shells. Add a No. 30 green rosette to toe.

2. On cookie sheet cover back and 1 side of second bootie with shells. Transfer to board and finish same as first one.

NOTE: If cake is to be transported you may prefer to set the booties on their side instead of upright. In this case the bottom (the sole) would be covered with yellow shells and the side resting on the board would be covered with a thin coat of frosting.

TO SERVE: Cut sweater into 16 pieces, hat into 2. Booties are 1 serving each.

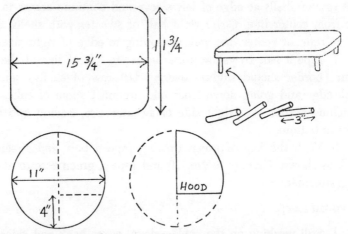

Fig. 34. Pattern for bassinet cake. Cut styrofoam ball in half as in-dicated by broken line, then cut 4" piece from bottom as indicated. This becomes the hood.

Bassinet Cake

Color plate 5   •   You will need:
    1 cake 12" x 17½" (3 recipes White Cake or two recipes Yellow Cake)
    1½ cups Decorator Frosting ½ cup blue; ¼ cup pink; ¼ cup green
    Prepared cake base (see fig. 34)
    Hollow styrofoam ball about 11" in diameter
    Ribbon and net for trimming base (satin blanket binding works as well, is less expensive)
    2 recipes Cherry, Strawberry or Blueberry Filling
    2¼ recipes Buttercream Frosting No. 1
    Corrugated cardboard about 12"x 16"
    Aluminum foil
    Piping gel
    2 ribbon pouf bows
    Plastic wrap and straight pins

One or two days before

Bake cake: Preheat oven to 325°. Grease bottom of pan and line with wax paper. Mix 2 recipes White Cake or 1 recipe Yellow Cake. Pour into prepared pan and refrigerate while you mix rest of batter. Bake about 1 hour 10 minutes or until cake tests done. Cool in pan on rack 15 minutes; turn out cake, remove paper and cool, top side up. Store until needed.

Make Decorator Frosting. Drop a No. 101 tube into small parchment cone. Fill with blue frosting and pipe out 3 small roses onto wax paper squares. Store roses and reserve remaining blue frosting.

Prepare base, trim with ribbon and net gathered together at edge and fasten with staples. Cut hood, fig. 34.

Early on party day

1. Make filling; cool. Make Buttercream Frosting.

2. Trace top of base on piece of corrugated cardboard. Draw another outline ¾" inside first; cut out on inside line. Cut a piece 4½" x 2" from remaining piece of cardboard.

3. Place the pieces of cardboard on cake and cut around them with a sharp knife. Trim smaller piece so it is only 1½" thick. Cover both cardboards with aluminum foil and place pieces of cake, top side up, on the foil.

4. Split large cake into two layers. Spread filling on lower one. Replace top layer. Give both cakes a thin coat of Buttercream to set crumbs. Let stand 20 minutes.

5. Spread piping gel on top of base; center the large cake on it with a ¾" margin all around.

6. Frost top of large cake and entire small cake smoothly with Buttercream. Using a string or straight edged spatula, make a line across the cake the short way, about 3" in from the end. Starting at this line and working downward to the opposite end of the cake, draw a line 2" in from the edge, all around, ending at the straight line across the top. (This will be guide line for the pink ruffle piped around the top.)

7. Color about ¾ cup of Decorator Frosting pink. Spoon into decorating bag and attach tube No. 104. Pipe a ruffle first around the cake over the guide line, then across the cake over line marked in frosting.

8. Set frosted pillow in place, centering it on cake between top ruffle and back edge. Be sure to leave room for the back edge of hood

behind pillow. Change to No. 16 on bag of pink frosting. Pipe a zigzag border around pillow and over the inside edge of ruffle.

9. Color remaining Decorator Frosting green. Use a parchment cone to pipe stems on pillow and coverlet.

10. Use blue Decorator Frosting and tube No. 101 to pipe tiny sweet peas. Arrange blue roses on stems as shown in photo. Cut cone of green frosting to a leaf tip and pipe the tiny leaves.

11. Press all but 2″ of three toothpicks into under edge of hood. Set hood in place, pushing ends of toothpicks into cake to hold it securely. Cover outside of hood with a thin coat of Buttercream.

12. Cover the entire hood with basket weave using Buttercream and tubes No. 6 and 48.

NOTE: You may mark the hood to help keep even vertical lines in the basket weave: Using a piece of string, mark a straight line at center of hood extending from front to back edge where it meets the cake. Add marks to both sides of the center one, keeping them ⅝″ apart at the front edge, closer together at the back. Mark all the vertical lines first, then start piping the basket weave at the left side of the hood and work as usual, piping the vertical lines over marks in frosting.

13. Starting at center back, cover body of bassinet with basket weave.

14 Pipe a No. 16 zigzag border at front edge of hood and a rope border around top edge of bassinet. If there is room around the cake base, you may pipe a rope border there also. Use Buttercream for all borders.

15. Cut two circles of plastic wrap the size of the pouf bows. Put pins into bows, through the wrap and then into place in styrofoam hood. (The plastic keeps Buttercream from staining bows.)

NOTE: Transport cake, if necessary, in a styrofoam cradle of the kind used for tier cakes on separators.

TO SERVE: Remove hood, cut cake into three lengthwise. Slice across into about 45 pieces.

Bar Mitzvah Cake

Color plate 6   •   You will need:
   1¼ cups Decorator Frosting colored blue
   1 book cake 8″ x 12″ (1 recipe Yellow Cake)
   corrugated cardboard 12″ x 18″
   gold foil doilies
   2 recipes Buttercream Frosting No. 1
   1 recipe Buttercream Filling Royale
   2 cups Chocolate Fudge Frosting
   16″ length sasheen ribbon
   gold foil leaves
   Bar Mitzvah Boy figure (See Sources of Supply)

Two days before

Make at least 3 roses on wax paper squares using blue Decorator Frosting and tube No. 126. Set aside to dry.

One day before

Preheat oven to 325° F. Grease bottom of book pan and line with wax paper. Bake about 1 hour or until cake tests done. Cool cake in pan on rack for 15 minutes. Turn out of pan, remove paper. Cool on rack *with rounded side up.*

Make Buttercream Frosting. Make Buttercream Filling Royale using 1 cup Buttercream as directed in recipe. Cover cardboard with doilies. (Be̅ sure channels in cardboard run across and not up and down.)

DECORATE:

1. Place cooled cake on doily covered board. Split into two layers, carefully remove top part. Spread filling over lower part, replace top.

2. Frost cake smoothly with Buttercream. Make page markings on the sides by running a metal decorating comb across. (For best results, dip comb into hot water first.) Also hold it at a 45° angle, off to the side, rather than at right angles to cake.)

3. Pipe No. 16 shell border around top of cake.

4. Pipe the rope border around the bottom with Chocolate Fudge Frosting and No. 30.

5. Slightly thin ¼ cup Chocolate Fudge Frosting and use with

a No. 2 tube to pipe on inscription. Place roses and leaves opposite inscription.

6. Put ribbon in place for book mark. Set figure on cake after it has been placed on table.

TO SERVE: Cut as shown for 9" x 13" cake in figure 26g.

French Poodle Birthday Cake

Color plate 7 • You will need:

> 12" x 17½" sheet cake (1 recipe Butter Cake)
> Picture of French poodle (6" x 8" or larger); ours came from a birthday card
> 1 sheet wafer paper 8½" x 11"
> 1 recipe White Whipped Buttercream (reserve 1 cup, color remainder pink)
> Piping gel: 1 tablespoon black, 1 tablespoon brown, 1 teaspoon pink, ¼ cup blue

Day before

BAKE CAKE. Preheat oven to 325°. Grease bottom of pan and line with wax paper. Mix batter as directed in recipe. Bake for 50 to 55 minutes or until cake tests done. Cool in pan on rack 10 minutes. Remove from pan; peel paper from bottom. Turn right side up on rack to cool. Wrap and store.

Prepare White Whipped Buttercream.

Trace picture of poodle on wafer paper. Cut out. Paint with white Buttercream as described under Wafer Paper Decorations, chapter 6. Mix black color into 2 teaspoons white Buttercream to make gray and use to touch up darker areas. Finish poodle completely using colored gel, but do not add bows and flowers.

On party day

Color reserved cup of Buttercream as follows: 2 tablespoons blue, 3 tablespoons green, 2 tablespoons purple, 2 tablespoons red, 2 tablespoons yellow, and 1 tablespoon brown.

FINISH CAKE:

1. Set cake on tray or covered cardboard rectangle. Rewhip But-

tercream frost and border, using pink Buttercream and No. 30 tube for the shell border.

2. Place colored poodle on cake, pressing edges into frosting. Pipe on bows with tube No. 101 and blue Buttercream. Pipe on drop flowers with pink and a No. 30 tube.

3. Add inscription, using blue gel and a No. 2 tube.

4. Fill a parchment cone with green Buttercream; cut tip to about the size of a No. 4 tube. Pipe stems of varying lengths as shown.

5. Add small blue, purple, yellow and red flowers using Buttercream and tubes No. 16, 30 and 140.

6. Cut parchment cone used for stems to a leaf tip. Add leaves to stems.

Sweet Sixteen Cake

Color plate 8 • You will need:
  1 12" x 17½" sheet cake (1 recipe Butter Cake)
  1 large tray or 14" x 22" foil-covered caterers' board
  1 recipe White Whipped Buttercream (colored pink)
  1 cup Decorator Frosting (½ cup green, 6 tablespoons red, 2 tablespoons yellow)
  16 small pink birthday candles and holders
  smilax or huckleberry foliage (optional)

Day before

Preheat oven to 325° F. Grease bottom of pan and line with wax paper. Prepare batter as directed and bake cake 50 to 55 minutes or until done. Cool in pan on rack for 10 minutes. Turn out of pan, remove paper and continue to cool, top side up.

Make patterns for numerals from paper or light cardboard. Number *1* should be 2½" thick and 11" high; the *6* should be 2½" thick, 7½" wide overall and 11" high.

Place cooled cake on cookie sheet, bottom side up. Lay pattern on cake and secure by driving straight pins through it and into the cake. Carefully cut around patterns with a sharp knife. Remove leftover cake and freeze for future use or frost to match Sweet Sixteen cake and use for additional helpings. Transfer numerals to board and remove pins and patterns. Cover top and sides with a thin coat of Buttercream to set crumbs.

On the day

1. Frost numerals smoothly with pink Buttercream. Pipe a No. 16 shell border top and bottom, using pink Buttercream.

2. Fill a parchment cone with green frosting. Pipe a curved vine with short stems coming from it as seen in the color plate.

3. Drop a No. 140 tube into a parchment cone and fill with red frosting. Use to pipe small flowers on stems. Add small yellow dots in center with a small parchment cone.

4. Cut cone of green frosting used for stems to a small leaf tip. Pipe leaves on stems.

5. Put candles into holders and arrange on cake. Add border of leaves.

TO SERVE: Cut across numerals into about 30 slices.

Cascade-of-Chrysanthemums Cake

Color plate 9 • You will need:
    1 recipe Decorator Frosting
    1 10″ tube cake (1 recipe Chiffon Cake)
    1 recipe Buttercream Frosting No. 1 colored yellow
    leftover pieces of cake

Two days before

Make Decorator Frosting. Color ¾ cup green, set aside. Use remaining frosting to make 12 to 15 chrysanthemums in various colors. See instructions for achieving the different color effects in the lesson on chrysanthemums. Choose your own colors or duplicate those in the color plate. Allow the mums to dry till needed.

Day before

Bake and cool cake as directed in the recipe. Place on cake plate or stand, *bottom side up*. Frost cake smoothly with Buttercream.

Build the foundation for the flowers as shown in figure 11a. Complete the cake as directed in Cascade-of-Flowers Cake.

Use reserved green frosting in parchment cone for stems and leaves.

Pipe a No. 30 shell border only around base of cake.

Pansy Birthday Cake

Color plate 10 • You will need:
  1¼ recipes Decorator Frosting
  1 14″ square cake (1¼ recipes Chiffon Cake)
  2 recipes Buttercream Frosting No. 1
  ½ recipe Chocolate Fudge Frosting
  2″ x 3″ piece of wafer paper
  2 tablespoons brown piping gel

About 1 week in advance

Make Decorator Frosting, set 1 cup aside. Use remaining frosting to make about 24 pansies in a variety of colors. Allow to dry.

One or two days before

Preheat oven to 325° F. Prepare pan by greasing bottom and lining with wax paper. If your mixer bowl isn't large enough to hold 15 cups of batter proceed as follows. After egg yolk mixture and egg whites have been beaten separately, combine in a large pot and fold together. Pour the batter into baking pan and bake about 1 hour 10 minutes or until cake tests done. Let cake hang suspended about ½ hour, then loosen around edges and turn out on a rack. Remove wax paper and cool cake, top side up.

NOTE: If cake seems loose in pan while it is hanging, remove it immediately and cool on rack as directed.

On the day

1. Make Buttercream and Chocolate Fudge Frosting.
2. Place cake, top side up, on large tray or doily-covered cake board.
3. Frost top of cake smoothly with Buttercream. Apply a thin coat of Buttercream to sides. Fill decorating bag with Buttercream and attach No. 16 tube. Use to striate sides. Change to No. 30 and pipe a shell border top and bottom.
4. Using a toothpick, mark a rectangle 6″ x 3½″ on cake, keeping the line 1½″ from bottom and 4″ from either side.
5. With tubes No. 6 and 48 pipe a basket over rectangle, using

Chocolate Fudge Frosting. Change to No. 16 and pipe a shell border around bottom and sides of basket.

6. Color reserved cup of Decorator Frosting green. Fill a small parchment cone and cut the tip off to about the size of a No. 4 tube. Pipe slightly curving stems, starting at edge of basket and working upward. The stems toward outside of basket should curve further outward.

7. Cut cone to a small leaf tip and pipe leaves at end of some of the stems.

8. Arrange pansies on the cake starting at top of stems. Continue adding flowers and working downward toward the top of basket, overlapping some for a more natural effect. Pipe dots of frosting under some of the pansies to secure and elevate them. Let a few flowers overhang the top of the basket.

9. Pipe additional leaves into arrangement, tucking them into spaces here and there between or under flowers.

10. Pipe inscription on wafer paper using brown gel. Tuck one corner between flowers as shown.

Daffodil Birthday Cake

Color plate 10 • You will need:
>1 recipe Decorator Frosting
>1 10" round cake baked from 1 recipe Genoise
>1 recipe White Whipped Buttercream
>1 jigger Creme de Cacao
>1 recipe Buttercream Filling Royale
>¼ cup brown piping gel
>3 miniature marshmallows, cut crosswise

Three days before

Make Decorator Frosting. Color ¾ cup green and ¼ cup orange. Color remaining frosting yellow, use to make 8 daffodils on wax paper squares. Finish centers with orange, set aside to dry until needed.

Day before or early on day

1. Bake and cool cake. Make White Whipped Buttercream. Use 1 cup in Buttercream Filling Royale. Save remainder to frost cake later.

2. Split cooled cake lengthwise making two layers. Sprinkle cut surface of both layers with Creme de Cacao. Spread filling over one

cut surface. Place cut surface of second layer over filling. Place cake on serving plate bottom side up. Frost smoothly with Buttercream.

3. Pipe a rope border top and bottom using Buttercream and tube No. 30.

4. Add brown gel inscription using tube No. 2 in a small parchment cone.

5. Pipe curved stems with No. 6 and green frosting. Place a half marshmallow on the stems at each point where a flower will be set. Cover marshmallow with green frosting pressed through No. 6. Carefully arrange daffodils on cake, tilting them at lifelike angles on marshmallows.

6. Fill a parchment cone with green Decorator Frosting and cut to a leaf tip. Pipe leaves as shown in photograph.

Double Bell Cake

Color plate 11 • You will need:
    4 bell-shaped layers (2 recipes White Cake or Sponge Cake)
    1½ cups Decorator Frosting
    1½ recipes White Whipped Frosting
    1½ recipes Almond or Walnut Cream Filling
    4 Royal Icing bluebirds (see Sources of Supply)
    14" x 22" foil-covered caterer's board or large tray

Day before

Preheat oven and prepare pans as directed in recipe. Bake 2 layers and remove from pans. Repeat for remaining 2 layers. Allow all cakes to cool thoroughly. Cover with clean towel.

Color 1 cup Decorator Frosting yellow. Make 4 roses and 8 corsage roses (see instructions for Vase of Roses cake, color plate 14.) Make White Whipped Buttercream; refrigerate.

Early on day

Make filling; cool. Remove Buttercream from refrigerator; rewhip.

Spread cooled filling between layers of both cakes. Place on board as shown in photograph with cakes touching at top only. Cover both cakes with a thin coat of Buttercream. Let stand about 20 minutes, then frost smoothly.

TO DECORATE:

1. Pipe a shell border top and bottom using Buttercream and tube No. 30.

2. Color rest of Decorator Frosting green. Use some in a small parchment cone with tube No. 6 to pipe stems on left side of both bells, as seen in Color Plate 11.

3. Place roses on stems; tilt them attractively.

4. Fill a small parchment cone with green; cut to a tiny leaf tip. With cone of green and No. 6 tip pipe tapered bulbs of frosting at bottom of corsage rose. Add tiny sepals with cone cut to leaf tip. Blend base of bulbs of frosting into stems by stroking with a wet water color brush.

5. Cut cone to a larger leaf tip and pipe leaves on the stems.

6. Press bluebirds into frosting on both cakes. Refrigerate until ready to serve.

NOTE: Almond Cream and Walnut Cream Fillings require refrigeration. If you are unable to refrigerate the cake, it would be best to choose another filling.

TO SERVE: Cut each lengthwise, then into five parts; 20 slices.

Vase of Roses Cake

Color plate 11 • You will need:
    picture of vase about 8" tall; ours came from magazine
    8½" x 11" sheet wafer paper
    ¼ cup blue piping gel
    1½ cups Decorator Frosting, 1 cup pink, ½ cup green
    2 round 12" cakes (1 recipe Butter Cake)
    2 recipes Orange Date Filling
    1½ recipes Buttercream Frosting No. 1 or Creamy Frosting

Two days before

Trace picture of vase on wafer paper and cut out. Place on cookie sheet or piece of cardboard and spread with a coat of blue piping gel using an icing spatula. Set aside to dry. Reserve extra blue gel.

Make 2 roses and 1 corsage rose from pink frosting. To make corsage rose start out as for full-bloomed rose until you have piped center cone and first three petals. Then skip second row of petals entirely and proceed to the last row. Start the petals (you will need only three) at the nail, bringing the top to just below the edges of the first row, then down to the nail again. Before removing rose from nail, taper the base by cutting excess frosting away with a wet paring knife.

Day before

1. Bake and cool cake as directed in recipe. Make filling and frosting. Place first layer on plate or board, top side down. Spread with cooled filling.

2. Frost cake smoothly and pipe a No. 30 shell border top and bottom.

3. Place vase on left side of cake, pressing edges into frosting. Fill a small parchment cone with blue gel. Cut tip to about size of No. 4 tube. Pipe inscription and line below it. Also use to pipe diagonal lines over vase. Cut tip on the cone larger and use to pipe the beading trim at top and bottom of vase.

4. Drop a No. 6 tube into a small parchment cone and fill with about ¼ cup green frosting. Use to pipe stems as seen in color plate.

5. Roll a second cone and fill with remaining green frosting. Cut to a tiny leaf tip. Put roses into place at ends of stems, tilting them at attractive angles. Pipe tapered bulb of frosting at base of corsage rose and center rose using tube No. 6. Bring end of bulb down over stem. Blend ends into stems by stroking with a wet water color brush. Pipe sepals on roses using green and the cone cut to a leaf tip.

6. Cut the leaf tip larger and add leaves to the arrangement.

Flag Cake

Color plate 12 • You will need:
    1 sheet cake, 12″ x 17½″ (1 recipe Butter Cake or 2 recipes
      Yellow Cake)
    1½ recipes White Whipped Buttercream; color ⅔ cup deep blue,
      2 cups bright red
    2 No. 47st tubes
    piece of wafer paper 5½″ x 5½″

Day before

Preheat oven to 325° F. Grease bottom of pan and line with wax paper. Mix batter, pour into pan. Bake 50 to 55 minutes or until cake tests done. Cool on rack in pan 15 minutes. Turn out of pan, remove paper, cool top side up. Cut cake to measure 11" x 13½".

Make and color Buttercream. Place cake bottom side up on tray or doily-covered board. Cover top and sides with thin coat of white Buttercream.

DECORATE:

1. Drop a No. 47st into a bag and fill with red Buttercream. Drop second 47st into another bag and fill with white.

2. Holding tube No. 47st flat side up, pipe a red stripe across the bottom of cake.

3. Pipe a white stripe directly above red one. Continue alternating one red and one white stripe until you have piped three of each.

4. Place square of wafer paper on a cookie sheet. Spread with coat of blue frosting. Carefully transfer to upper left hand part of cake above last stripe piped.

5. Continue piping alternate-colored stripes, starting them at the edge of blue field, until you have piped seven red and six white stripes. They should cover the entire top of the cake.

6. Attach a No. 16 tube to a bag of white Buttercream. Striate sides of the cake and finish off top edge with any desired border.

7. Pipe white stars on blue field with No. 16, starting with 5 evenly spaced rows of 6 across. Then pipe 4 rows of 5 across in between the first rows of stars.

First Class Male Cake

Color plate 12   •   You will need:
  piece of wafer paper, 1½" x 2½"
  1 sheet cake 9" x 13" (1 recipe Ice Water Fudge Cake)
  1 recipe Creamy Frosting
  ¼ cup black piping gel
  2 tablespoons red piping gel
  ¼ cup blue piping gel

Two days before

Make stamp of wafer paper by tracing any small design and painting with piping gel. Set aside to dry.

One day before

1. Bake and cool cake as directed in recipe. Make frosting. Place cake on tray or doily-covered board, bottom side up. Frost smoothly and apply No. 30 shell border to *bottom only.*

2. Using a small glass or cookie cutter, mark circle about 2″ in diameter for postmark. Put stamp into place in upper right corner of cake.

3. Fill a small parchment cone with black piping gel and cut a very tiny piece from end. Use to outline and letter the postmark and to pipe cancellation marks across stamp.

4. With red piping gel and a No. 2 tube, write *First Class Male* under stamp.

5. Using blue piping gel and No. 2 tube, address cake to the recipient and write the name and address of donor in upper left corner.

Golf Cake

Color plate 13 • You will need:
   1 round 10″ cake (1 recipe White Cake or Ice Water Fudge Cake)
   1½ recipes Buttercream Frosting No. 1
   2 tablespoons blue piping gel
   Candy Pebbles
   ½ cup green Decorator Frosting
   Golf Set (see Sources of Supply)
   ¼ cup red piping gel

One day before

Bake and cool cake. Make Buttercream. Split cooled cake lengthwise making two layers. Spread cut surface of cake with Buttercream. Cover with second cake placing cut surface over filling. Transfer to cake plate, bottom part of cake up.

1. Frost cake and pipe a No. 30 shell border using Buttercream. (Reserve ½ cup.)

2. Color ½ cup reserved Buttercream green. Use in a small parchment cone with No. 6 to fill in green area on cake. Dip finger into warm water and smooth frosted area.

3. Make lake by filling in small area with blue gel squeezed from a parchment cone as described above but *do not* smooth with finger. Border the lake with candy pebbles.

4. Pipe trees with No. 30 and green decorator frosting. Hold tube touching the cake surface and straight up. Exert heavy pressure on bag and gradually raise tube. When the tree is about 1½″ tall, discontinue pressure and pull tube away.

5. Put golfer, flag and ball into place on cake.

6. Fill a small parchment cone with red gel; cut tip to about size of a No. 4 tube. Use to pipe dots between shells in the top border and to outline the bottom border.

NOTE: You can make cakes for other sports too (see Sources of Supply for equipment). The basketball cake is made from a 9″ x 12″ sheet.

Crown Cake for Father's Day

Color plate 14 • You will need:
　　1 recipe Chiffon Cake baked in 10″ tube
　　1 recipe Creamy Frosting
　　toothpicks
　　silver dragees
　　6 diamonds of wafer paper, 2¼″ x 1″ each
　　½ cup red piping gel
　　¼ cup blue piping gel
　　12 green jelly beans

Day before

1. Bake and cool Chiffon Cake as directed in recipe. Make frosting. Place cake on footed cake stand *top side up.*

2. Space 6 toothpicks evenly around outside edge of cake. Press a toothpick between each two, 1″ below top edge. Place 6 toothpicks around the hole in center of cake, lining them up with the ones around the outside edge.

3. Using toothpicks as guides, cut 6 points around the top of the cake. Remove toothpicks.

4. Frost cake. Fill decorating bag with frosting and attach a No. 16 tube. Border top edge of cake with a row of flat stars. Make certain to center star on each point and improve edge lines if possible.

5. Center a silver dragee on each star using a tweezer.

6. Mark a line around lower part of cake, 1″ above the plate. Fill a parchment cone with red gel and cut to about size of a No. 4 tube. Striate a band around the cake between the mark and the plate.

7. Pipe a row of No. 16 stars at each edge of the band. Center a silver dragee in each star.

8. Place 3 wafer paper diamonds on a cookie sheet. Spread with a coat of red piping gel. Carefully transfer them to cake, leaving a space between each two. See color plate.

9. Spread remaining 3 diamonds with blue gel. Place on crown in spaces between the red ones.

10. Border each diamond with No. 16 stars and place silver dragee in the center of each.

11. Place 2 green jelly beans, one above the other, between the diamonds.

Petits Fours

Color plate 15
The flowers made in advance from Royal Icing using tubes No. 16, 101, 30, 131 and 140. Lines and stems were piped with tubes 2 and 4. A parchment cone cut to a leaf tip (fig. 19) was used for the leaves.

Chrysanthemum Thanksgiving Cake

Color plate 16   •   You will need:
  2 recipes Decorator Frosting
  2 round 12″ cakes (1 recipe Butter Cake)
  2 recipes Mixed Fruit Filling
  2 jiggers Light Rum or Peach Brandy
  1½ recipes Creamy Frosting or Buttercream Frosting No. 1
  ¼ cup brown piping gel
  4 miniature marshmallows

At least 3 days before Thanksgiving

Make Decorator Frosting. Color ¾ cup green, cover and set aside. Color ½ cup each of yellow, purple, and bronze (mix yellow, orange and brown together). Make 1 chrysanthemum from each color. Scrape remaining frosting of each color into a separate saucer. Combine with some remaining white frosting to make other color combinations. Make some flowers by striping cone with color. (See figure 17 for the different effects possible.) You will need 8 mums in all but if possible make extras so you can choose the ones that complement each other best. The extras can be stored for future use. Set flowers aside to dry.

Day before

1. Bake and cool cakes as directed in recipe. Make filling and frosting. Split cooled cakes in two making two layers from each. Place first layer on serving plate cut side up. Sprinkle with about ⅓ the rum or brandy; then spread with ⅓ the cooled filling. Repeat until you have piled 4 cake layers with 3 layers of filling between and used all the rum or brandy. Be sure to use the bottom half of 1 layer at the top. Let cake stand ½ hour.

2. Frost cake and pipe No. 30 shell border top and bottom.

3. Pipe the inscription using brown gel and No. 4 tube.

4. Add 4 curved stems with green frosting and No. 6 tube.

5. Snip marshmallows in half and place 1 piece wherever you will place a mum. Cover them with green squeezed from No. 6 tube.

6. Fill a parchment cone with green and cut to a leaf tip. Add leaves to stems.

7. Arrange chrysanthemums on stems, tilting them on the marshmallow pieces.

8. Pipe additional leaves if needed to complete the arrangement.

Cornucopia Thanksgiving Cake

Color plate 16 • You will need:
   Fruit molded from Fondant (see index)
   1 round 10″ cake (1 recipe White Cake)
   1 recipe Blackout Filling
   1 recipe White Whipped Buttercream
   1 ice cream cone (sugar, not waffle type)
   1 recipe Decorator Frosting and paste colors
   ¼ cup brown piping gel

In advance

Make fondant fruit as far ahead as convenient; store until needed.

Day before Thanksgiving

1. Bake and cool cake. Make filling and frostings.

2. Split cake lengthwise making two layers. Spread cooled filling between layers. Place cake on prepared plate or base.

3. Frost cake smoothly with Buttercream. Pipe a shell border top and bottom using Buttercream and tube No. 30.

4. Color 1½ cups Decorator Frosting yellow, then add enough

brown to make a straw color. Frost ice cream cone about three-quarters of the way around, leaving an unfrosted strip about 1" wide at the mouth of the cone, tapering to nothing at the point.

5. Place cone, unfrosted side down, on a cookie sheet. Use remaining straw-colored frosting and tubes No. 6 and 48 to pipe basket weave over the cone. Pipe a No. 16 rope border around the mouth of the cone with the same frosting. Allow to dry slightly.

6. Pipe inscription on cake with tube No. 4 and brown piping gel.

7. Place the cornucopia (ice cream cone) on the cake at an attractive angle, leaving room for the fruit.

8. Arrange fruit on cake as follows: Start farthest away from the mouth of the cornucopia and work back to it. Pile the fruit highest at the mouth of the cornucopia by adding more layers of fruit there and less away from it. It may be necessary to pipe small dots of Buttercream between some fruits to hold them in place. The arrangement need not be symmetrical but should give the illusion of spilling out of the cornucopia.

9. Color the remaining Decorator Frosting green. Stripe a small parchment cone with brown paste color, then fill with green frosting. Cut the cone to a leaf tip and use to pipe leaves between and around fruit.

Poinsettia Christmas Cake

Color plate 17 • You will need:
    1 recipe Decorator Frosting
    1 round 10" cake baked from 1 recipe White Cake
    1 cake plate or doily-covered cake board at least 12" in diameter
    1 recipe Pineapple Filling
    1 recipe Buttercream Frosting No. 1
    ¼ cup red piping gel
    2 tablespoons blue piping gel
    2 tablespoons yellow piping gel

At least four days in advance

Make Decorator Frosting. Color 1 cup bright red. Use to make poinsettias. (You will need four but make extras to allow for breakage.) Color remaining Decorator Frosting as follows: ½ cup yellow (for centers of poinsettias and candles), ¼ cup orange (for centers of poinsettias), ½ cup green (for leaves).

Day before or on day

1. Bake and cool cake. Make Pineapple Filling and Buttercream. Split cake into two layers. Fill with cooled filling and set on plate. Frost smoothly with Buttercream Frosting.

2. Pipe shell border top and bottom with tube No. 30 and Buttercream.

3. Pipe inscription with No. 4 in a parchment cone and red piping gel.

4. Use No. 6 and yellow frosting for candles. Pipe the longest one in center first, then pipe two more candles to either side of the first one, graduating them in size. Make flames with a small parchment cone and blue gel. Add glow marks around flames with yellow gel in a small parchment cone.

5. Arrange poinsettias over the candles, piping bulbs of Buttercream under them for support if necessary.

6. Add leaves around poinsettias using green frosting and a parchment cone cut to a leaf tip.

Party Cookies

Color plate 18

The cookies pictured were trimmed with Royal Icing in various colors piped through a No. 2 or No. 4 tube. A few were first spread with cookie glaze, then trimmed. The birds, fish and the blankets and caps on the elephants were painted with Royal Icing first, then trimmed as described previously. Facial features were piped with No. 2 while other accent lines were added with a No. 4.

Confirmation Cake

Color plate 19 • You will need:
1½ cups Decorator Frosting (1 cup red, ½ cup green)
An oval cake (1 recipe White Cake)
1 recipe Orange-Date Filling
1 recipe White Whipped Buttercream
2 tablespoons Buttercream colored blue
oval of wafer paper about 2½" x 1"
1 small white sugar or plastic dove
2 tablespoons gold piping gel
¼ cup brown piping gel

Three days before

Make and color Decorator Frosting. Make two roses on wax paper squares using red frosting and tube No. 104; reserve balance of red and all of green frosting.

Day before

Preheat oven to 350° F. Grease bottom of 7¾" x 11" x 2¾" oval pan and line with wax paper. Mix batter as directed, bake about 45 minutes or until cake tests done. Cool as directed in recipe. Make filling and Buttercream frosting.

DECORATE:

1. Place cake on oval tray of doily covered cardboard about 4" larger than cake. Split cake into two layers. Spread bottom layer with filling, cover with top layer, cut surface down.

2. Frost cake smoothly and pipe on a No. 30 shell border top and bottom.

3. Frost oval of wafer paper with blue Buttercream. Place on cake as seen in color platé 18. Press dove into frosting on oval. Fill a small parchment cone with gold gel and pipe glow marks around oval.

4. Pipe inscription with brown piping gel and tube No. 2.

5. Fill a parchment cone with green frosting and cut tip to about the size of a No. 4 tube. Use to pipe stems on cake.

6. Set roses in place. Drop a No. 104 tube into a parchment cone and fill with red Decorator Frosting. Pipe sweetpea-like flowers on stems as shown in color plate.

7. Cut cone used for stems to a leaf tip. Pipe a leaf at the base of each sweetpea and a few around the roses.

TO SERVE: Cut lengthwise then across for about 20 slices.

Shamrock Cake

Color plate 19   •   You will need:
> shamrock pattern
> picture of a Leprechaun about 5" tall. (see figure 20)
> 5" x 3" piece of wafer paper
> ¼ cup green piping gel
> 1 teaspoon gold piping gel
> 1 teaspoon pink piping gel
> 1 teaspoon white frosting
> 1 teaspoon black gel
> 1 12" square cake (1 recipe Yellow Cake)
> 1 recipe Creamy Frosting colored green

Anytime before

Make shamrock pattern by cutting a paper heart about 5" high by 4¾" wide. Trace heart pattern three times on a larger piece of paper to form a cloverleaf. Add stem to bottom. The shamrock should measure about 11" overall.

Trace the picture of the Leprechaun on wafer paper and cut out. Finish as described under Wafer Paper Designs using piping gel and white frosting. After the face and hands have been painted add a bit of red color to the pink gel and use for the nose. Set aside to dry.

Day before

Bake and cool cake as directed in recipe. Make Creamy Frosting, color green.

Place cooled cake on cookie sheet or heavy cardboard, bottom side up. Lay pattern on cake and drive straight pins through it into cake to secure in place. Carefully cut around pattern using a sharp knife. Transfer shamrock to a tray or doily-covered cardboard circle about 14" in diameter. Cake scraps may be used for nibbles or stored in freezer for future use in puddings etc.

Cover top and sides of cake with thin coat of frosting to set crumbs. Allow to stand overnight.

THE FOLLOWING DAY:

1. Frost cake and add a No. 16 shell border top and bottom using green frosting.

2. Place Leprechaun in center of cake as seen in the color plate. Press edges gently into frosting.

3. Fill a small parchment cone with remaining green gel. Cut tip off to about the size of a No. 4 tip. Use to pipe inscription.

TO SERVE: Cut as round cake, about 12 to 16 servings.

Washington Log
Color plate 20 • You will need:
 2 Jelly Rolls
 Tray or cake board about 20" long
 1 recipe Chocolate Fudge Frosting or Chocolate Buttercream
 1 cupcake
 Maraschino cherries on stems
 Green wafer paper leaves

Day before
1. Make Jelly Rolls as directed in recipe. You will only need 1½ for the Log so cut one Roll in half. Store 1 piece in the freezer for future use.

2. Make Chocolate Frosting. Place the whole Roll on tray, cover one end with frosting. Press cut end of the half Roll against frosting making a long Log. Frost completely.

3. Cut top of cupcake off at an angle and press at side of Log near the top to give the effect of a short branch. Cover with frosting.

4. To achieve the look of bark, run the tines of a fork over the frosting vertically in uneven lines. It will be easier if the fork is dipped into hot water from time to time.

5. Garnish with cherries and wafer leaves.

Refrigerate until serving time.

TO SERVE: Cut across into about 16 slices.

Box of Roses
Color plate 20 • You will need:
 2 recipes Decorator Frosting, color 3 cups pink, balance green
 4 sheets Cake for French Pastry (see Index for recipe)
 2 recipes Buttercream Frosting No. 1
 1 recipe Chocolate Buttercream
 piece of masonite 4½" x 23½" x ¼" or ⅜"
 2 cups finely chopped nuts or grated semi sweet chocolate
 5" x 24" rose box from florist
 ribbon and matching pouf bow (optional)
 florist card (optional)

Three days ahead

With pink frosting and No. 126 tube, pipe about 18 roses as follows: Make rose on nail as usual until you have piped cone and first three petals. Skip second row of petals entirely. Start third row at base of cone as usual but bring tube up to almost the top of the first row of petals, then come down to base of cone again. You will only need three or four petals to complete the last row. While rose is still on nail, taper base by cutting away excess frosting with paring knife which was first dipped into hot water. Remove rose from nail and place on cookie sheet. Gently push rose over on its side and allow to dry in this position. You will need only twelve roses but make extras so you can choose only the perfect ones.

Day before

1. Bake the 4 sheets of cake as directed in the recipe; cool. Make Buttercreams, cover masonite with aluminum foil. Place first sheet of cake on cookie sheet top side up. Spread with half the Chocolate Buttercream. Top with second sheet of cake, spread with 1½ cups Buttercream Frosting No. 1. Cover with third sheet of cake and spread with remaining Chocolate Buttercream. Cover with last sheet of cake, *top side up.* Trim edges of cake evenly on all four sides.

Cut two strips 4" wide from length of cake. Transfer first strip to masonite board, leaving a ¼" margin on three sides. Measure length of strip on board. Cut enough from second strip so combined length of the two will be 23". Spread some buttercream at one end and press the two pieces together on board.

Color Buttercream pale green (the color of the inside of the florist box) if desired. Frost the top and sides of the cake. Press chopped nuts or grated chocolate around the sides of the cake. Open one end of the rose box and slide the cake into it; close box again.

TO DECORATE:

1. Attach No. 6 tube to decorating bag and fill with green Decorator Frosting. Pipe 12 rather straight stems on cake, long in the center, slightly shorter on either side. The remaining 9 stems are about the same length.

2. Change to No. 4 tube and pipe short stems "growing" from the longer stems.

3. Put first rose into position on center (long) stem. Change back to No. 6 on bag of green and pipe a tapered bulb of frosting at base of rose, ending at stem. Brush end into stem with a wet watercolor brush to blend.

4. Fill a small parchment cone with green Decorator Frosting and cut to a small leaf tip. Add tiny sepals on first rose. Caution: Be sure to add bulb and sepals to each rose as it is placed on cake.

5. Continue putting roses in place, one at a time, and finishing bases as described previously.

6. When all roses are in place, cut the leaf cone larger. Add 5 leaves (one at tip and two to either side) to each short stem.

If desired, tie top of box with ribbon and fasten bow as shown in color plate. Card, if used, may be stuck under ribbon.

NOTE: I have used Buttercream Frosting No. 1 because the inside of my florist box was pale green, one of the few colors this buttercream will take successfully. It is not essential to match the color of the box but if you wish to use any color but pale green, White Whipped Buttercream would be a better choice since it takes all colors beautifully.

TO SERVE: Cut as loaf cake; about 24 slices.

Easter Hat and Purse Set

Color plate 21 • You will need:
    25 Royal Icing drop flowers (pink or yellow)
    1 recipe White Cake
    1 recipe White Whipped Buttercream
    1 12″ corrugated cardboard circle
    1 hat stand or footed cake plate
    1 8″ x 10″ piece corrugated cardboard
    ½ cup brown piping gel
    1 cup green Decorator Frosting
    1 strip nylon net 1½″ x 10″

At least three days before

Make drop flowers from 1 recipe of Royal Icing as far ahead as desired. Use brown gel for dots in centers.

The day before

1. Preheat oven to 350° F. Grease and flour one 8″ x 8″ x 2″ pan

and a bowl about 5" in diameter. Choose a bowl with a nice round bottom for crown of hat.

2. Mix White Cake as directed in recipe. Measure 3½ cups of batter into square pan; pour remaining batter into bowl. Bake 20 to 25 minutes or until cakes test done. Cool in pans on rack for 10 minutes then turn out on racks top side up and cool.

3. Make Buttercream, cover and store in refrigerator till needed.

Early the next day

1. Remove Buttercream from refrigerator, allow to stand at room temperature 20 minutes. Meanwhile fasten cardboard circle to hat stand or cake plate with a few dabs of piping gel. Cover cardboard rectangle with foil or fasten a greaseproof doily to it with piping gel. Cut the 8" cake to a 6" x 8" rectangle.

2. Beat Buttercream to restore fluffiness. Color yellow, then add a little brown to make straw color.

3. Cover corrugated circle with a coat of Buttercream. Set round cake, flat side down, about 1½" in from back edge of circle keeping it an equal distance from both sides. Press round cake down gently to secure in place. Cover round cake with a coat of Buttercream, set aside.

4. With a skewer or similar instrument, punch a hole in center of cardboard rectangle. Punch four more holes, one on each side, about 2" in from edges. Spread a small amount of Buttercream in center of rectangle and place 6" x 8" cake on it. Secure cake to board by pressing toothpicks through holes in board, inserting them from bottom; break them off even with top of cake. (You may omit this step if you do not intend to present the cake with purse propped against hat stand as shown.)

5. Cover the rectangular cake with Buttercream, set aside.

COMPLETE THE HAT CAKE:

1. Using a string or small spatula, mark a straight vertical line in center of frosted crown. Attach a No. 16 tube to a decorating bag and fill with Buttercream. Pipe first row of straw design over this line as follows. Exert gentle but steady pressure on bag as it is moved in a side-to-side motion, starting at lower back edge of crown and continuing to lower front. Start second row of straw design to right of

first. Continue until entire right half of crown is covered, keeping rows close together.

2. Turn cake around and cover other half with straw design.

3. Cover entire brim with straw design, starting at back close to base of crown and working around it. Make the last row almost vertical and over the thickness of the corrugated cardboard to give a finished look to the brim.

4. Drop a No. 48 tube into a parchment cone and fill with brown piping gel. Pipe a band around the crown where it meets the brim, starting and ending at center back.

5. Press drop flowers over hat band as shown, spacing them slightly over 1" apart.

6. Fill a parchment cone with green Decorator Frosting and cut to a leaf tip. Pipe leaves between the flowers.

COMPLETE THE PURSE CAKE:

1. Cover the two short sides of purse with vertical rows of straw design, then cover bottom with horizontal rows. Starting at top left corner and working across, cover front of purse with straw design.

2. Place strip of nylon net on a piece of wax paper. Cover with lengthwise rows of straw design, leaving an uncovered margin of ¼" at each end. Slide knife blade under strip at center, and lift the strip from wax paper. If necessary, slide blade in one direction or another and bring loose ends together. Press unfrosted loose ends into upper right corner of purse, allowing looped end to rest on cardboard.

3. Press drop flowers into place as shown in the photograph. Pipe leaves between flowers.

NOTE: Purse may be propped up against the hat stand when cake is placed on party table.

TO SERVE: Cut round cake into 4 wedges, other lengthwise first, then into slices. 16 servings in all.

Lamb Cake

Color plate 22 • You will need:
    A cake baked in a lamb mold (1 recipe Old-Fashioned Pound Cake)
    1 recipe Mock Marshmallow Frosting
    large oval tray or foil covered cardboard
    12 ounces coconut
    2 packages jelly beans

Day before

Mix, bake and cool cake as directed for bunny, but pour batter into the *face half* of mold. Fill mold to within ⅛" from the top.

1. Apply frosting as described for bunny. Paint inside front of ears with pink frosting *after* sprinkling with coconut.

2. Make necklace on lamb with half jelly beans.

3. Finish cake plate as described for bunny, using jelly beans in place of marshmallow eggs.

TO SERVE: Slice across; about 10 servings.

Bunny Cake

Color plate 22   •   You will need:
    8 or 9 blue Royal Icing drop flowers
    1 cake baked in a rabbit mold (1 recipe Old-Fashioned Pound Cake)
    large oval tray or corrugated board covered with foil
    1 recipe Mock Marshmallow Frosting
    12-ounce package coconut
    2 pink jelly beans
    package of assorted color marshmallow eggs

Three days before

Make drop flowers if you don't have any on hand.

Day before

Preheat over to 300° F. Grease and flour mold very carefully to cover all surfaces. Place half of mold on cookie sheet.

Mix batter as directed in recipe. Pour about 3 cups into mold half on cookie sheet; batter should come to within ⅛" of top of mold. If desired, lay toothpicks on batter at weak points (ears, neck etc.) Put other half of mold in place, being sure it fits tightly. (Extra batter may be used for cup cakes.)

Put cookie sheet with mold on it into oven. Bake about 1 hour 15 minutes. Carefully remove top half and insert cake tester. If not done, replace mold and bake a little longer.

When cake is baked, place mold on cake rack; carefully remove top but leave cake in lower half until completely cold. Loosen cooled cake at edges and place a cake rack over it. Invert rack and mold. Lift mold from cake and leave cake on its side on rack. Trim away any uneven cake at bottom so bunny will be level when it is turned up on end.

DECORATE:

1. Make frosting. Spread small amount in the center of prepared plate or cardboard. Stand bunny upright on frosting, pressing down gently.

2. Fill decorating bag with frosting and attach No. 16 tube. Squeeze frosting all over bunny except for a thin strip in middle of each ear. (I have found this method easier because it gives a better coverage and shows more contours than when the frosting is applied with a spatula.)

3. Sprinkle coconut over frosted bunny.

4. Mix a bit of pink color into about 1 tablespoon of frosting Use with a brush to paint unfrosted part of ears.

5. Snip slightly less than half from a pink jelly bean with a scissors. Press into frosting for bunny's nose.

6. Snip about ⅓ from each end of second jelly bean. Use for eyes. Paint part of eyes nearest front with brown color.

7. Pipe dots of frosting behind drop flowers and press them around neck for a necklace.

8. Color remaining frosting and coconut green. Thin frosting slightly by blending in a small amount of water. Brush over cake plate around bunny and out to edge of plate.

9. Press colored eggs into frosting, forming a border around the plate. Sprinkle green coconut between egg border and bunny, covering green frosting.

10. Plate remaining eggs over the coconut around bunny.

NOTE: For instructions on how to color coconut see directions for Locomotive Cake, plate 1.

TO SERVE: See serving suggestions for Lamb Cake.

Easter Egg Cake

Color plate 23 • You will need:
> 4 white Royal Icing Rabbits (see Figure Piping-Pattern Method, fig. 22)
> 1 cake baked in egg cake mold (1 recipe Old-Fashioned Pound Cake)
> oval platter or foil covered cardboard
> 1 recipe Chocolate Fudge Frosting
> ¾ cup White Whipped Buttercream (½ cup yellow, ¼ cup green)
> package of jelly beans
> 1 cup coconut, colored green

Three days before Easter

Make rabbits.

Day before

Preheat oven to 300° F. Grease and flour both halves of egg cake mold; place on cookie sheet. Mix cake as directed in recipe. Pour about 2 cups batter into each half of the mold. (Unlike lamb and bunny, egg cake is baked in two parts. Use extra batter for cup cakes.)

Bake egg cake about 50 minutes or until cake tester inserted in center comes out clean. Allow to stand in mold on rack until cold. Level tops with a very sharp knife before turning out of molds. Turn out on racks *flat side down.*

1. Place half of cake on oval platter or doily-covered cardboard, flat side up. Spread with Chocolate Fudge Frosting. Cover with second half, rounded side up.

2. Frost egg completely. If you wish a smooth shiny surface do the following: Heat about ¾ cup frosting over low heat to just lukewarm. Pour or spoon over the frosted egg, spreading quickly with small spatula. Allow coating to set for 1 hour.

3. Scrape away any coating that may have run down on the plate.

4. Fill a decorating bag with yellow Buttercream and attach a No. 16 tube. Pipe a shell border around egg where the two halves come together.

5. Change to No. 2 and pipe the inscription.

6. Fill a small parchment cone with green and cut tip to about size of a No. 4 tube. Pipe lines as seen in color plate.

7. Press rabbits into place on egg.

8. Sprinkle area around egg with green coconut. Scatter jelly beans over coconut.

TO SERVE: Slice across; about 10 servings.

Easter Cross Cake

Color plate 24   •   You will need:
  ½ recipe Royal Icing
  1 cross cake 12″ x 17″, baked in a cross pan or cut from a sheet cake
   (see figure 2*d*)
  1¼ cups Decorator Frosting; 1 cup green, ¼ cup yellow
  yellow paper stamens (about 60)
  2 recipes Buttercream Frosting No. 1 or 1½ recipes White Whipped
   Buttercream colored yellow

At least three days before Easter

Make lilies from ½ recipe of Royal Icing. They are fragile, so it would be well to make more than the 7 you will need. After they have dried, and before they are removed from nails, pipe yellow centers with No. 6 and Decorator Frosting. Press 5 paper stamens into each lily.

Day before

Bake cake using any desired recipe. You will need about 12 cups of batter for cross pan or 12″ square pan. (Check the batter yield of recipe you choose.) Bake at 325° F. unless your recipe specifies lower temperature. Test for doneness before removing from oven. Cool cake thoroughly, top side up.

Make Buttercream; if you are using Buttercream Frosting No. 1 add color slowly, as too much will give a curdled appearance. Prepare board or cake plate.

FINISH CAKE:

1. Place cake on tray, bottom side up. Apply thin coat of Buttercream to sides. Frost top smoothly.

2. Fill decorating bag with Buttercream and attach a No. 16 tube. Striate sides of cake.

3. Pipe shell border top and bottom with No. 16 and Buttercream.

4. Pipe long slightly curving stems, using green frosting and No. 6.

5. Fill parchment cone with green frosting; cut to a leaf tip. Add leaves to stems, making them smooth and tapered by *not* working the hand from side to side as they are formed.

6. Arrange lilies as seen in color plate. With tube No. 6 and green frosting, add tapered bulb to base of each lily, bringing end down over stem. Blend the ends into stems by stroking with wet watercolor brush.

NOTE: If you prefer chocolate frosting use about 2 recipes either Chocolate Buttercream or Chocolate Fudge Frosting.

TO SERVE: Cut as a loaf cake; about 40 slices.

Panorama Eggs
Color plate 25

Mold and assemble eggs as described under Sugar Molding, then decorate as follows using Royal Icing:

1. Pipe the large shell borders with tube No. 30 and the smaller ones with No. 16.

2. Stems, where used, are added with tube No. 4.

3. The drop flowers are made with No. 131 and the centers are added with No. 16.

4. No. 101 is used for the tiny sweet peas.

5. The bow is piped with No. 101.

6. The rabbits are piped with No. 4 as described under Figure Piping, Pattern Method.

7. Pipe the leaves with a parchment cone cut to a leaf tip.

Sugar-Molded Ducks
Color plate 25

Mold ducks as described under Sugar Molding. Allow to dry, then put halves together with Royal Icing to form full figure. Allow the Royal Icing to set 12 hours before decorating. Decorate with Royal Icing following directions below.

Boy Duck

1. Paint shirt front with white icing.
2. Paint coat with blue icing and edge with blue, piped through No. 4 tube.
3. Squeeze crown of hat through the coupling without using a tube. Pipe brim with a No. 101.
4. Paint eyes with white, then dot front of them with black.
5. Crease crown slightly with dull edge of a table knife after frosting has set about 10 minutes.
6. To prevent bleeding of color, allow to dry before adding red hatband, tie and buttons. Use tube No. 4.
7. Paint beak with orange icing.

Girl Duck

1. Paint beak and eyes as described for boy duck.
2. Paint shawl with pink. Edge with a No. 101 ruffle in pink, pipe top edging and ties with No. 4.
3. Paint top of head with pink for a hat. Edge with No. 16 flat stars. Trim with No. 30 flat stars.

Wedding Cake trimmed with fresh flowers

Color plate 26 • You will need:
   3 round two layer tiers, 6", 10" and 14" (2 recipes Butter Cake)
   3 recipes Apricot Filling
   3 recipes White Whipped Buttercream
   Base for cake
   4-5 Sweetheart roses, 3 spider mums for arrangement; 8 extra
      Sweetheart roses and pieces fern for base.

Three days before wedding

Preheat oven, prepare pans and mix 1 recipe Butter Cake as directed. Pour batter to a depth of 1" in 6" and 10" pans. Pour remaining batter into 14" pan; refrigerate. Bake the 6" cake about 20 minutes and the 10" one about 30 minutes. The 14" cake will require about 50 minutes baking time. If the batter has been refrigerated it will of course require longer baking time. In any case it is always best to test a cake before removing it from the oven. After first three cakes are removed from the pans, mix second recipe of Butter Cake and repeat as described above.

Next morning (Two days before wedding)

In morning, make filling and Buttercream. Prepare base for cake. I used a 16″ plywood circle with Tuk 'n' ruffle (see Sources of Supply) stapled to it.

In evening, spread filling between layers. Place each cake on corrugated circle; give each cake a thin coat Buttercream.

One day before wedding

In morning, frost and assemble two lower tiers as explained under Wedding and Tier Cakes.

Make flower arrangement: Stuff highball glass with water-soaked floral foam (Oasis). Make outline of design with foliage, fill in outline with small roses and spider mums. Refrigerate to keep flowers fresh.

Cut a hole in the center of the 6″ tier large enough to hold glass with floral arrangement. Frost tier and put into place on other two.

TO DECORATE THE TIERS:

1. Use No. 6 and Buttercream for the string work on all tiers.
2. Mark garlands on second tier and pipe them with No. 16.
3. Make garlands on lowest tier in the same way but use No. 30.
4. Pipe all shell borders except lower one on bottom tier) with tube No. 30. Use pastry tube No. 5A (star tube) for border around the bottom.
5. On wedding day, insert glass holding flower arrangement into hole in top tier. Cover exposed glass with basket weave using Buttercream and tubes No. 6 and 48.
6. Cut all but 1″ from the 8 rose stems and discard pieces. Wrap stem on each rose in wet cotton, then in aluminum foil. Space roses around base of cake; add fern leaves in between.

TO SERVE: See cutting directions figure 26; 75 servings.

Bridal Shower Cake

Color plate 27 • You will need:
　　1 cake, 10" round (1 recipe White Cake)
　　1½ recipes Decorator Frosting (1 cup pink, 1 cup blue, ¼ cup yellow,
　　　remainder green)
　　1 recipe Grape, Blueberry or Strawberry Filling
　　Wafer paper, about 5" x 8"
　　1½ recipes Buttercream Frosting No. 1
　　¼ cup brown piping gel

Two days before

Bake cake. Make Decorator Frosting. Make 3 roses on wax paper squares using No. 126 and pink frosting. Set aside to dry. Make top of umbrella (fig. 20), using wafer paper. Cut out. Store decorations and frosting.

On the day

1. Make filling and Buttercream frosting.

2. Thin about ½ cup blue Decorator frosting with a small amount of egg white or white corn syrup. Spread evenly over wafer paper umbrella top. (You may not need all the frosting for this.)

3. Split cake into two layers. Spread filling between layers; place on cake plate or doily covered board, bottom side up.

4. Frost smoothly with Buttercream. Pipe a No. 30 shell border top and bottom.

5. Pipe inscription with brown piping gel and a small parchment cone as shown. Turn cake so inscription is centered perfectly.

6. Carefully transfer frosted umbrella to cake, centering it under inscription. Mix thinned blue frosting with other blue and fill decorating bag.

7. Pipe handle and spike at top of umbrella with blue frosting and No. 12. Change to No. 101 tube and pipe ruffles at lower edge of umbrella starting with the lower ruffle.

8. Pipe bow on handle using No. 48 (flat side up) and pink frosting.

9. Fill small parchment cone with green frosting and cut tip to about the size of a No. 4 tube. Pipe curved stems on cake.

10. Arrange roses at center of stems as shown.

11. Change to No. 140 on bag of blue frosting. Pipe forget-me-nots into arrangement. Use yellow frosting in a cut parchment cone for dots in the center.

12. Cut parchment cone used for stems to a leaf tip. Add leaves to the arrangement as shown.

Mortarboard Cake

Color plate 27 • You will need:
    2 cake layers, 8" each (1 recipe White Cake)
    1 recipe Orange Filling
    1 recipe White Whipped Buttercream
    1 10" square corrugated cardboard
    1 fluted paper cup cake liner

On the day

1. Bake and cool cakes as directed in recipe. Make filling and frosting. Place first layer on cake plate, bottom side up; spread with filling. Top with second layer, bottom side up.

2. Remove ½ cup Buttercream to small bowl. Color remaining Buttercream blue and use some to frost top and sides of cake.

3. Center cardboard on top of round cake. Frost top and edges of cardboard with blue.

4. Fold fluted cup into eighths to form wedge shape for tassle. Push straight pin into point of folded cup and into side of cardboard to fasten them together.

5. Fill small parchment cone with blue and another with white Buttercream. Cut off to about size of No. 4 tube. Pipe strings to tassle starting at center top of hat out to edge. Continue down folded cup to bottom. Alternate a few strings of each color until entire folded cup is covered. Overlap strings at top of hat and spread them over folded cup so tassle will be tapered.

6. Cut tip on cone of blue to about size of a No. 6 and pipe a button at center top of hat over start of tassle.

NOTE: Colors may be changed to those of school but I suggest that you use chocolate rather than lots of black frosting which, in large doses, is less palatable.

Doll Cake

Color plate 28 • For doll trimmed in blue you will need:
    1 recipe Old-Fashioned Pound Cake or White Cake
    removable angel-food core
    2 recipes Orange or Lemon Filling
    1 recipe White Whipped Buttercream Frosting
    1 teen-age-type doll, 8" tall

Day before

Preheat oven as directed in cake recipe. Grease and flour removable core, one 2-quart ovenproof bowl, 8" or 9" in diameter, and a layer cake pan of about the same size.

Mix batter; pour into layer cake pan to a depth of slightly under 1" if using Pound Cake and slightly over that if using White Cake. Center core in bowl; fill with remaining batter. Bake layer cake about 20 minutes, bowl cake about 50 minutes. Test both before removing from the oven. Cool in pans on racks for 10 to 15 minutes. Turn out of pans and cool layer cake top side up and bowl cake round side up.

NOTE: If you do not have removable core, an empty can from 6-ounce fruit juice concentrate may be used. Wrap sides with aluminum foil and fill with rice or dry beans to weight it. Grease and flour outside before using.)

On day

1. Make filling and frosting.

2. Place cake layer on serving plate, trimming level top if necessary. (Reserve pieces of cake.) Spread layer with filling, using slightly more than half.

3. Level bowl cake if necessary, then split lengthwise into two layers. Place bottom layer, (flat one) over filling. Spread remaining filling over top of second layer. Top with last piece of cake, round side up.

4. Insert doll and frost as described under Doll Cakes. Extra cake may be used to hold doll in hole securely if needed.

FINISHING CAKE:

1. Tint two cups of Buttercream blue. Mark off skirt into 8 equal sections by scratches started at cake plate and extending upward

about 3½″. Use a cold meat fork or some similar instrument to make parallel scalloped grooves ¼″ to ⅜″ apart. see figure 27c). These grooves serve as guidelines for piping ruffles.

2. Pipe a row of flat No. 30 stars around bottom of skirt where it meets the cake plate, using white Buttercream.

3. Fill decorating bag with blue Buttercream and attach No. 104 tube. Starting at bottom pipe ruffles over grooves marked in frosting, completing 1 row before going on to next. If you must stop to twist bag or refill it, be sure to do it at end of the scallop as break won't show there. The thick end of the 104 should touch grooves as you work hand back and forth, but thin end should stand away and point downward.

4. Finish the top edge of the last row of ruffles with blue Buttercream and a No. 16 used in a side-to-side motion.

5. Add a tiny blue dropped loop with No. 4 at each point between scallops. Finish top of each loop with small circle of frosting similar to button border, using No. 16 and blue Buttercream.

6. Pipe blue belt around waist, ending it in a small bow with streamers at back; use No. 4 and blue Buttercream.

7. Finish top edge of bodice with tiny No. 16 stars.

8. Color about 2 tablespoons Buttercream red. Press out two No. 30 flowers at waist. Color a small amount of Buttercream yellow and add dots to center of flowers.

9. Mix green color into about 2 tablespoons Buttercream. Use in a parchment bag cut to a leaf tip to add tiny leaves around the flowers.

TO SERVE: Remove the doll. Cut across about 3½″ from the bottom. Slice top layer into 8 or 10 pieces; bottom into 10 or more slices.

Doll Cake

Color plate 28   •   For doll dressed in pink, you will need:
   1 8″ teen age type doll
   1 recipe Old-Fashioned Pound Cake or White Cake
   removable angel-food core
   1 recipe Almond or Walnut Cream Filling
   1 recipe White Whipped Buttercream
   1 small snap on type plastic bottle cap about 1¼″ in diameter
   piece of flexible cardboard 2¼″ x 1″

Day before

Mix, bake and cool cakes as described for doll trimmed with blue.

On day

Follow steps 1, 2, 3 and 4 (doll dressed in blue). Remove I cup Buttercream to another bowl. Color remainder pink for step 4. Paint long sleeves and high neckline on bodice.

FINISHING CAKE:

1. Mark center front with a straight line starting at neckline and extending to cake plate.

2. Fill decorating bag with white Buttercream and attach tube No. 16. Make fur effect by using tube in a side-to-side motion on either side of line at center front. Continue in a single line around bottom of cake.

3. Trim sleeves edges and add a fur collar using white Buttercream and No. 16.

4. Staple strip of cardboard into a cylinder for muff. Slip over doll's hand as shown and cover with white fur using No. 16.

5. Fasten bottle cap to head with corsage pin. Cover with fur using white Buttercream and No. 16.

NOTE: Keep cake refrigerated because Cream Fillings are very perishable.

TO SERVE: See serving suggestions for Doll Cake trimmed in blue.

Bride Doll Cake

Color plate 28 • You will need:
   1 recipe Yellow Cake
   2 recipes any filling sufficient for a 10″ cake
   1 recipe White Whipped Buttercream
   1 teen-age-type doll, 10″ tall
   strip cellophane or plastic wrap 3″ x ½″
   ¼ cup green piping gel
   3″ piece florist wire
   pearls or crystal beads
   5″ circle nylon net

Day before

Preheat oven to 325° F. Grease and flour a 2 quart ovenproof bowl about 9″ in diameter and angel food core. Grease bottoms and line with paper 2 10″ round pans. Pour batter into 10″ pans to a depth of about 1″; refrigerate. Pour remaining batter into bowl and bake about 50 minutes. Cool as directed for doll cake trimmed in blue. Raise oven setting to 350° F. for 10″ cakes. Bake about 50 minutes. Test before removing from oven because time may vary with refrigerated batter. While cakes are cooling make Buttercream and filling.

Put layers and bowl cake together with filling as described for doll cake trimmed with blue. Drop doll into hole in center. Frost cake and paint bodice with white Buttercream as described under Doll Cakes. Sleeves should be painted to the wrist and end in a point on the hands.

TO FINISH THE CAKE:

1. Drop tube No. 126 into decorating bag. Fill with Buttercream and pipe ruffle around bottom of skirt.

2. Attach coupling and No. 30 to another bag and fill with Buttercream. Mark guidelines for the trim on the skirt using a pin or toothpick starting at the waist and working down. Pipe over the lines working the tube in a side to side motion.

3. Mark trim from waist up to neckline on bodice. Change to No. 16 and pipe in same way as the trim on skirt.

4. Press strip of cellophane or plastic wrap between doll's arm and body, bridging the gap. Pipe 6 or 8 stems in graduated lengths over the strip with a parchment cone and green gel.

5. Change to No. 101 on the bag of white and pipe tiny sweet peas at the ends of the stems. Cut the cone to a leaf tip and add tiny leaves to the stems.

6. Change to No. 4 tube and pipe a white bow and streamers on the bouquet.

7. String beads on florist wire, twist ends to form a ring. Sew nylon net to ring for veil. Place on doll's head and fasten into place with small hairpins.

TO SERVE: Remove doll; cut across twice making three layers. Cut each layer into 10 or more pices.

Pink Wedding Cake

Color plate 29 • You will need:

    1 recipe Royal Icing

    3 recipes Decorator Frosting

    18″, 14″, 10″ and 6″ tiers, two layers each. Butter Cake, White Cake or Yellow Cake may be used. See table on p. 21 for amounts of batter. The 18″ tier will probably need to be pieced from smaller cakes. It may be omitted altogether for smaller cake. In this case reduce filling by ¼ and White Whipped Buttercream by ⅓.

    8 recipes Apricot Filling

    6 recipes White Whipped Buttercream

    Silver foil leaves

    Cake ornament

About 1 week before

Make at least 4 medium-sized butterflies as described under Lattice Work using Royal Icing. If time permits make extras in case of breakage.

Make at least 16 roses using tube No. 126. You will also need about 125 partially opened roses made as described in Box of Roses Cake but using tube No. 104.

Three days before

Bake and cool cakes. Make filling and frosting; refrigerate. Trim tray or board.

Two days before

Fill cakes. Color Buttercream pale pink. Spread a thin coat on cakes.

One day before

Frost and assemble cakes as directed under Wedding and Tier Cakes.

DECORATE AS FOLLOWS:

1. Using tube No. 6 and Buttercream pipe string work on two top tiers. Add No. 16 rope border top and bottom.

2. Mark guidelines for garlands on third tier using string work or

a cookie cutter. Pipe garlands with No. 30. Add double drop strings above them with No. 6.

3. Apply No. 104 ruffle around bottom tier then add garland with No. 30. Use No. 6 for double dropped strings.

4. Pipe No. 30 rope border top and bottom of third tier and at top of last tier. Use pastry tube 5A for shell border around bottom of cake.

5. Press partially bloomed roses between drops and at corners of top tier.

6. Place butterflies on second tier as shown.

7. Start clusters of roses at bottom and work upward to top edge of tier. Place a large rose at top of each cluster; add large and small silver foil leaves.

NOTE: To simplify the design omit clusters of roses on the bottom tier, using just the large roses at edge.

TO SERVE: See cutting directions figure 26; 210 servings from 4-tier cake; 90 servings from 3-tier cake.

Daisy Wedding Cake

Color plate 30   •   You will need:
   2 recipes Royal Icing
   ½ cup yellow Decorator Frosting
   4 round two-layer tiers, 7″, 10″, 13″ and 16″ (4 recipes Butter Cake or
      9 recipes White Cake)
   4 recipes Pineapple Filling
   4 recipes White Whipped Buttercream
   Silver tray or trimmed cake board at least 22″ in diameter
   36 1¼″ green wafer paper leaves
   4 bunches white cloth lily-of-the-valley
   Top ornament (see Sources of Supply)

One week before wedding

Make about 60 daisies on wax paper squares from white Royal Icing. Pipe centers of yellow Decorator Frosting. Allow to dry uncovered for 2 days, then store covered.

Three days before wedding

Bake cakes. See chart for amounts of batter to use. If you prefer not to measure batter, proceed as follows: Pour batter to a depth of about 1½" in 16" pan. Have batter in other pans 1" deep. (Extra batter may be used for cup cakes.) Approximate baking times: 16" cake about 50 minutes, 13" cake 40 to 45 minutes, 10" cake about 30 minutes, and 7" cake about 20 to 25 minutes (test to be sure.) These times are for batter which has *not* been refrigerated. Refrigerated batters take longer baking times.

Two days before

In the morning, make filling; cool. Make Decorator frosting. Spread filling between layers, put each tier on a corrugated cardboard circle. Cover each cake with thin coat of frosting to set crumbs. Store cakes in cool place overnight.

One day before

In the morning, frost and assemble cake completely; decorate as follows:

1. Use a No. 6 tube and Buttercream for all string work.

2. Pipe garlands on third tier with tube No. 30 and Buttercream.

3. Change to tube No. 48, serrated side up, and pipe garlands on lowest tier. Pipe elongated No. 30 shells between garlands.

4. Use No. 16 for shell borders on two upper tiers, No. 30 for remaining ones (except for border at base of the lowest tier. Change to pastry tube—star tube—No. 5 for this one.)

TO MAKE THE SPIRALS OF DAISIES:

1. Mark a line in frosting starting at base border on left side of lowest tier, continuing diagonally up to top border on right side. Turn cake around and repeat so marks start and end opposite each other.

2. Using tube No. 30, pipe some Buttercream into setback between tiers (over the guideline) to help spiral climb more smoothly.

3. Begin arranging daisies at cake plate and working upward over guideline. Have some flowers overlap each other slightly. Pipe extra Buttercream under daisies where necessary to hold them to cake securely, pressing them gently but firmly against cake.

4. When all daisies are in place, add leaves and lily-of-the-valley to complete spirals.

Engagement Cake

Color plate 31 • You will need:
    1 recipe Decorator Frosting, colored pink
    diamond-shaped corrugated cardboard 19″ x 15″
    2 yards silver Tuk n Ruffle (optional; see Source of Supply)
    1 recipe Yellow Cake, baked in diamond-shaped pan
    1 recipe any filling sufficient for a 10″ cake
    1 recipe Buttercream Frosting No. 1
    heart cutter about 3¾″ in diameter
    1 bottle silver dragees
    ¼ cup brown piping gel
    Engagement ring and box (from novelty store)

Three days before

Make about 75 pink drop flowers using tube No. 131. Set a silver dragee into the center of each using tweezer. Store reserved remainder of pink Decorator Frosting. Staple Tuk 'n' Ruffle to board or use a large tray.

Day before or on day

Preheat oven as directed in recipe. Grease bottom of 15″ x 10″ x 3″ diamond-shaped pan and line with wax paper. Be sure to follow directions for how to get level cakes (otherwise sharp points will thin cake in corners). Mix batter and bake as directed for 12″ square cake. Cool; make Buttercream Frosting and the filling.

Place cake on prepared board, bottom side up. Split into two. Remove top layer; spread cut side of bottom layer with filling. Replace top layer, cut side over filling. Frosting cake smoothly with Buttercream. Pipe string work around sides using tube No. 6 and pink Decorator Frosting.

With heart cutter, mark two hearts on cake. Cover marks with rather flat No. 16 stars and Buttercream. Set silver dragee in the center of each one. Use brown piping gel and No. 2 tube to pipe names on the hearts. Place open box containing ring above hearts.

Carefully arrange drop flowers around cake edge to form border.

Pipe a No. 16 rope border around the bottom of cake using Buttercream.

NOTE: This can also be used as anniversary cake; inscribe the number of wedded years with silver dragees.

Ice Cream Bombe
Color plate 32

1. Chill mold in freezer for 1 hour.
2. Pack firmly with ice cream. Place a piece of buttered wax paper over top before twisting cover onto mold. Return to freezer.
3. Whip 1 pint heavy cream. (color if desired)
4. Drain 4 slices canned pineapple on paper towels. Cut in half, making 2 semi-circles from each.
5. Shell and coarsely chop pistachio nuts to make ¾ cup.
6. Prepare a large serving plate or tray.
7. Unmold bombe by dipping quickly in and out of hot water. Remove cover and wax paper from top. Place serving plate over mold and invert. Lift off mold.
8. Spread whipped cream quickly over bombe, keeping indentations as much as possible. If bombe begins to melt, return it to the freezer for a few minutes to firm up.
9. Arrange pieces of pineapple around base of frosted bombe.
10. Attach No. 5A tube to 14" decorating bag and fill with whipped cream. Swirl cream around top of bombe as a garnish.
11. Press pistachios into indentations; sprinkle nuts over swirl at top of bombe as a garnish.
12. Pipe large whipped cream rosette in center of each pineapple piece. Return to freezer until serving time. To serve, cut with a knife which has been dipped into very hot water.

VARIATION: Line bottom and sides of mold with a 1" thick coat of ice cream. Freeze until firm. Fill cavity with ice cream or sherbet of another flavor. Seal mold and freeze as directed above. After unmolding, frost entire bombe as directed above or garnish base and top with whipped cream rosettes or sugared violets.

Dessert Buffet
Color plate 33

Strawberry Shortcake

1. Bake two 8" layers from ½ recipe Yellow or Sponge Cake; cool.
2. Whip 1 pint heavy cream until stiff.
3. Wash and hull 1 pint strawberries. Reserve large, perfect ones for garnish. Slice others and combine with about ¼ of the whipped cream. Spread between the layers.
4. Frost cake with remaining whipped cream. Finish sides with

decorating comb if desired. Garnish top with berries. Scatter extra berries around the cake plate as shown.

Chocolate Nut Torte (page 55)

Coffee Cream Pie

1. Make a 9" pie shell from your favorite recipe. Bake and cool.
2. Fill with Coffee Cream Filling.
3. Garnish with whipped cream piped through a No. 5A tube.

Glazed Fruit Pie

1. Prepare, bake and cool a 9" pie shell.
2. Fill with fruit and cover with glaze as described in recipe for French Tarts.
3. Garnish with whipped cream piped through a No. 16 tube.

Sandwich Loaves
Color plate 34

All three loaves are frosted and decorated with cream cheese. See Chapter 10 for complete instructions.

SOURCES OF SUPPLY

Try department store Gourmet shops for some of the special ingredients (such as candy pebbles and sugared violets) called for, but for equipment you will probably need one of the following suppliers. Write for information and catalogs.

Kitchen Glamor
15300 Fenkell Avenue
Detroit, Michigan 48227

Maid of Scandinavia Company
3245 Raleigh Avenue
Minneapolis, Minnesota 55416

H. Roth and Son
1577 First Avenue
New York, New York 10028

Wilton Enterprises
833 West 115 Street
Chicago, Illinois 60643

Wolly's Incorporated
310 Main Street
Farmingdale, New York 11735

INDEX

223

blackout, 79
blueberry, 82
buttercream royale, 78
cherry, 83
chocolate custard cream, 80
coffee custard cream, 80
custard cream, 79
grape, 81
lady baltimore, 79
lemon, 81
maple walnut cream, 80
mixed fruit, 81
mocha, 80
orange, 82
orange date, 81
pineapple, 78
strawberry buttercream, 79
flag cake, 189
flour, 16
 amount to use at high altitudes, 29
flouring pans, 22
 for baking at high altitudes, 29
flower nails, 87, 89
flowers, 102-119
 black-eyed susans, 109
 chrysanthemums, 116
 daffodils, 111
 daisies, 109
 decorating cakes with, 90
 drop, 102
 forget-me-nots, 104
 gumdrop, 156
 lilies, 118
 pansies, 106
 poinsettias, 119
 roses, 114
 sweet peas, 104
flowers made of frosting, drying, 169
folding ingredients, 30
fondant fruits, 159-162
fondant icing, easy, 76
fondant, making, 159
 molding fruit from, 159
food coloring for frosting, 66
food decorating, 149
forget-me-nots, 104
 plate 2, 95
freehand figure piping, 125-130
 clowns, 126
 rag dolls, 130
 Santa Claus, 130
freezing cakes, 24, 169
freezing decorated cakes, 25, 169
 frosted cakes, 25
 plain cakes, 24

French pastry, 45
French tarts, 47
frosting flowers, 169
frosting technique, 63
 amounts to use, 66
 spider web design, 65
 storing frosting, 66
 striating sides of cake, 65
 when buttercream looks curdled, 66
frostings
 chocolate buttercream, 72
 chocolate fudge, 77
 creamy, 73
 decorator, 72
 mock marshmallow, 74
 uncooked buttercream, 72
frosty nut crescent cookies, 61
fruit-filled chiffon cake, 42
fruit glaze, 77
fruit pie, glazed, 222
fudge cake, ice water, 38

garland with double dropped string, 137
 striated, 137
garland with ruffle, 136
garland with string, 137
garland with tassle, 136
garlands, 136
 plate 1, 94
 plate 2, 95
genoise cakes, 34
 failures with, 28
girl head, 132
glass pans, baking in, 21
glazed fruit pie, 222
glaze, chocolate cookie, 62
 cookie, 61
 fruit, 77
golf cake, 191
graduation cake
 mortarboard, 212
grape filling, 81
greasing pans, 22
 for baking at high altitudes, 29
gumdrop flowers, 156
 daisy, 156
 rose, 156
 tulip, 156

Halloween jack-o-lantern, 171
high altitude baking, 29
hints for decorators, 88
holly leaves, 121
how to color icing, 66
hyacinth salad, 153

practicing your decorations, 84
preparing to mix ingredients, 29
pricing cakes, 164
publicizing your services, 164
puffs, cream, 50

rabbits, 134
rag dolls, 130
rope border, 94, 97
roses, 114
   plate 5, 103
rosette border, 94, 97
royal icing, using, 74
royal icing with fresh egg whites, 75
royal icing with meringue powder, 75

salads
   candle, 151
   clown face, 153
   decorating molded vegetable, 155
   hyacinth, 153
   Santa Claus, 153
   tulip, 151
   waterlily, 153
sandwich loaf decorating, 149
sandwich loaves, 222
Santa Claus, 130
   salad, 153
separators in tier cakes, 146
shamrock cake, 198
shell border, 93, 94
shortcake, strawberry, 221
shortening, 16
shower cakes, baby
   bassinet, 178
   sweater set, 175
shower cakes, wedding
   bridal, 211
   bride doll, 215
sources of supply, 222
sour milk chocolate cake, 36
spatulas, icing, 87
spiced pound cake, 34
sponge cakes, 29, 31
   failures with, 25
sports cakes, 191
stabilized whipped cream, making, 154
stems, 120
strawberry buttercream, filling, 79
"strawberry" cookies, unbaked, 61
strawberry ice cream cake, 35
strawberry shortcake, 221

strings, making, 135
   plate 1, 94
   plate 2, 95
sugar, 17
   amount to use at any altitude, 29
sugar-molded ducks, 208
sugar molding, 162, 163
   panorama eggs, 162
summer coating, 76
suppliers, 222
sweet peas, 104
   plate 2, 95

tarts, French, 47
temperature, controlling oven, 23
temperature, oven, adjusting for high
   altitudes, 29
Thanksgiving cakes
   chrysanthemum, 193
   cornucopia, 194
tidbit tree, 154
tier cake, assembling a, 142
tier cake, making a, 141
tier cakes, using separators in, 146
tiger heads, 134
time, adjusting baking, 23
torte, chocolate nut, 55, 222
transporting tier cakes, 167
tulip salad, 151
two-toned petals, how to pipe, 107
turkey salad sandwich filling, 150

wafer paper decorations, 123
wafer paper designs, making, 124
Washington log, 199
waterlily salad, 153
wedding cake, assembling a, 142
wedding cake, making a, 141
wedding cakes
   daisy, 218
   double bell, 187
   pink, 217
   trimmed with fresh flowers, 209
whipped cream decorating, 149
whipped cream, making stabilized, 154
white cake, 35
white whipped buttercream frosting no.
   2, 71
writing aid, 140
writing on cake, 139

yellow cake, 37